BFI FILM CLASSICS

CÉSAR

. . . .

Stephen Heath

bfi Publishing

First published in 2004 by the
BRITISH FILM INSTITUTE
21 Stephen Street, London W1T 1LN

The British Film Institute
promotes greater understanding
and appreciation of, and
access to, film and moving image
culture in the UK.

British Library Cataloguing-in-Publication Data
A catalogue record for this book is available from the British Library

ISBN 0–85170–833–1

Series design by
Andrew Barron & Collis Clements Associates

Typeset in Fournier and Franklin Gothic by
D R Bungay Associates, Burghfield, Berks

Printed in Great Britain by Cromwell Press, Trowbridge, Wiltshire

CONTENTS

. . . .

INTRODUCTION

. . . .

'I regard Marcel Pagnol as the greatest cinematographic author of today,' declared Jean Renoir in 1937, the year following the release of *César*. It was not a view shared by other film-makers, for whom the commercial success of Pagnol's films seemed rather too evidently to represent the new talking film's abandonment of the art of cinema in the illegitimate interests of 'canned theatre', trading cinematic essence for theatrical convention. Pagnol himself did nothing much to discourage such a view; on the contrary, he developed an account of cinema as a medium whose purpose, seemingly, could be little more than to 'fix' theatre, a view which led to him being dismissed or ignored by generations of cinephiles and 'serious' filmgoers. 'Truth to tell,' commented *Cahiers du cinéma* in a survey of French directors twenty years after Renoir's accolade, 'one doesn't know what to think of him.'

Pagnol was indeed first of all a man of the theatre. The title credits at the beginning of *César* announce that the film 'brings to a close the Marseille trilogy begun with *Marius* and *Fanny* in 1929 and 1931'. *Marius* and *Fanny* were plays before they were films and the dates given are those

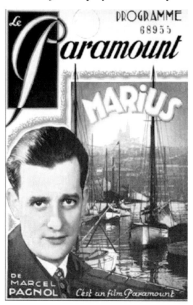

of the former, not of the latter. The films followed on the triumph of the plays: the 1929 play *Marius* became the 1931 film *Marius* directed by Alexander Korda; the 1931 play *Fanny* became the 1932 film *Fanny* directed by Marc Allégret (unless otherwise stated all subsequent references in this book are to the films of *Marius*, *Fanny* and *César*). *César*, however, marked a significant shift: a film before it was a play, it was written as a script and directed by Pagnol himself. In the period from *Marius* to *César*, the man of the theatre had gone over to the cinema (a 'betrayal' for which he was attacked by the theatre establishment). The commitment to cinema, moreover, was all-embracing: in the course of the 1930s, Pagnol established himself not just as a director but also as a producer and distributor, while simultaneously acquiring studios and processing laboratories. He conceived a future for the new cinema and set about obtaining the resources to allow him to help shape it.

The trilogy films were highly successful and immediately acclaimed as 'a great popular epic'. Though times have changed, their popularity remains and they have become part of the tissue of French culture; certain scenes and comic exchanges are general knowledge, strongly *familiar*. It was thus only natural that one of France's main television channels should choose to celebrate the year 2000 by commissioning expensive remakes of the three films: the trilogy is after all, in the words of television star Roger Hanin, the César of the remakes, 'a monument of the national heritage'.

If Pagnol did not direct the first two films, he was nevertheless very much their *author* and the trilogy overall is *his*. The cover of the programme for *Marius* consisted simply of the title, the name of the production company and a picture of Pagnol against an image of the film's Marseille port setting; this was, the programme announced, *Marius* 'de Marcel Pagnol'. It was the same with *Fanny*, again presented as a 'film de Marcel Pagnol', to Allégret's annoyance. *César*, the closing film, directed by Pagnol in his own studios, can to some extent stand alone but is everywhere informed by the events, characters, words and images of its predecessors. Audiences at the time of its release, and indeed thereafter, went to it with knowledge and expectations carried over from *Marius* and *Fanny*; they wanted to meet the characters again and see the drama resolved. As though to underline this, Pagnol was fond of recounting that he came up with the final storyline just as shooting was about to begin in response to the demands of an old lady who would only loan him furniture for one of the sets if he told her what happened next, thereby ensuring she would not die without knowing the drama's conclusion. Concerned with *César*, the film included in the 'BFI Film Classics' list, this short book must necessarily also be concerned with the trilogy overall. Just as Pagnol's old lady had to know what came after, so we, going the other way, have to know what came before, must look back to *Marius* and *Fanny*.

Authors of 'Film Classics' volumes often choose their film because of an attachment to it, some particular meaning it has for them. My choice is no exception. *César* has been with me since my early teens when I acquired long-playing records of scenes from the trilogy (how and why I no longer know). Later, I heard those same scenes many times on the radio and eventually saw the films themselves, seeing them several times again over the following years. Most recently, I watched them in the context of a growing interest in Marseille, the richly fascinating city to which they are so closely tied and which, like them, has given me a great deal of pleasure.

1

....

PAGNOL, CINEMA

Life

As he liked to recall, Pagnol was born in the same year as the cinema, within a few February days of the Lumière brothers' registration of the patent for their cinematic apparatus in 1895. His birthplace was Aubagne, a small town ten miles inland to the east of Marseille, where his *instituteur* father taught at the local school. Two years later, the family moved to the outskirts of Marseille and then in 1900 to the centre of the city itself where Pagnol grew up, spending childhood summers in La Treille, a village in the hills to the northeast – summers evoked in his memoirs *La Gloire de mon père* and *Le Château de ma mère*, widely known as a result of Yves Robert's 1990 film versions. After his primary schooling, he attended the Lycée Thiers (the location for his 1935 film *Merlusse*) where in 1914, with a group of friends he founded a literary review, *Fortunio*; short-lived in its first and second series, it was successfully relaunched in 1921, eventually becoming the influential *Cahiers du Sud* (though Pagnol's involvement had ceased before then). In the second series, Pagnol published two sonnets by another young Marseillais also to have a – very different – theatre and cinema career: Antonin Artaud.

After gaining a degree in English from the Université de Montpellier, Pagnol followed in his father's footsteps and became a teacher. He taught in schools in Tarascon, Aix and Marseille, until in 1925, at the age of thirty, he was given a post in the Lycée Condorcet in Paris. To reach the capital had long been his goal and this for reasons not of academic but of literary ambition. In 1927, he duly abandoned teaching to concentrate on making his breakthrough as a writer. This came the following year with the success of his play *Topaze*; a social satire in which a modest teacher is caught up in the world of business and gets the better of those seeking to manipulate him, but at the cost of the moral principles he had once sought to instil in his pupils. The success was confirmed a year later by the theatrical triumph of *Marius* and by the spring of 1930, the two plays together had totalled over a thousand performances in Paris alone. Such popular success was to accompany Pagnol throughout his career, and the more so after his turn to cinema.

Pagnol's interests and activities beyond his plays and films were multiple: translating Virgil and Shakespeare went along with attempts to prove Fermat's last theorem; skills at making things led to numerous inventions, some of which he patented, some of which were ingeniously improbable (an emergency braking system dependent on a giant foot dropping down to lift a car's wheels off the ground). Important for his cinema career was precisely this ability to turn his hand to anything and his determination always to succeed. Creative, commercial, practical and persuasive talents combined in a way that was decisive for the accomplishment of the turn to cinema.

In the first years of World War II, Pagnol continued his cinematic activities in Marseille (Marseille being in the 'free zone', not until late 1942 under German occupation), finishing *La Fille du puisatier* (1940), which had been interrupted by the outbreak of war, and beginning what was announced as his 'second trilogy', *La Prière aux étoiles*. Like the first, this was to comprise three films named after the three main characters but set mostly in Paris and in a quite different social milieu. The project was abandoned early in 1942 to avoid the films falling into the hands of the German-controlled Continental Film company, set up to run production and distribution in the occupied zone and increasingly exercising authority beyond it. One of the films had been more or less completed but Pagnol physically destroyed the copies (accounts, including Pagnol's own, vary as to how complete the destruction was and fragments survive; what I have seen of them, together with the published script, suggests that this second trilogy would have been embarrassingly bad).

The Liberation saw him in Paris at the head of a 'purification committee' established to look into the wartime activities of dramatic authors and composers, which he wound up quickly and painlessly. In 1942, given the situation in France, he had refused to stand for election to the Académie française but he agreed and was elected in 1946; an election heralded as that of 'the first Academician of cinema'. He died in 1974 and was buried in La Treille. The funeral oration was given by René Clair, himself by then a fellow member of the Académie and a long-standing friend, despite their sharp public exchanges in the 1930s over the introduction of sound.

Into Cinema

At the beginning of the 1930s, Pagnol was a powerful presence in French theatre; by the end of the decade, he had become a powerful presence in

French cinema. The moment is important: Pagnol's encounter with cinema was with the new *talking* pictures. Previously, he had shown little interest in film, not much beyond a couple of dissatisfied pseudonymous reviews in *Fortunio* and some half-hearted attempts to have a film made of an early play about boxing written with a friend (it eventually became Roger Lion's 1932 *Direct au cœur*). The advent of the talkies coincided with Pagnol's success as a playwright and it was this coincidence that prompted his quick enthusiasm. A recent arrival in the theatre world, he was without the prejudices of many established dramatists and more readily open to the possibilities of the new medium; coupled with which, his reputation facilitated his entry into cinema – he was after all the hot theatrical property of the day.

In characteristic anecdotal style, Pagnol many times described the encounter with cinema. Dining in a restaurant in Paris one spring evening in 1930, he was greeted by the actor Pierre Blanchar just back from London and full of the experience of seeing – and hearing - a talking film: 'the illusion is perfect, it's hallucinatory'. The film was *The Broadway Melody* (Harry Beaumont, 1929), featuring Bessie Love and showing at the London Palladium. Pagnol went to London the next day, saw the film three times, and returned to Paris 'enflamed with theories and projects'. He had no doubts: the future lay with the talking picture as 'the new mode of expression of dramatic art'; a conviction immediately proclaimed in an article for the newspaper *Le Journal* published under the title: '"The talking film" offers the writer new resources'.

The decisive first step towards Pagnol's appropriation of these resources was his meeting with Robert T. Kane, head of Paramount's European production arm, which had sound studios on the outskirts of the capital in Saint-Maurice where standardised versions of American films were made simultaneously in different languages for the various national markets. Kane appointed Pagnol to head an ephemeral 'literary committee' of French writers (Kane's relation to literature is summed up by his demand one day that the poet Verlaine, thirty years dead, be brought to his office immediately). More importantly, he allowed access to the studios where, with nothing particular to do, Pagnol spent his time moving from department to department, learning all he could about cinema. This apprenticeship was vital: 'If, later', he insisted, 'it was possible for me to make films, while at the same time directing a laboratory, studios, and distribution agencies, I owe it to the friendship of Robert T. Kane.'

Kane had acquired screen rights to the play *Marius*, the film of which would be by far the most successful of Paramount's small number of original European productions. Alexander Korda was brought in to direct, Pagnol provided the adaptation, and the film was shot in five weeks in 1931 (Swedish and German versions were shot at the same time, the German version also directed by Korda). The shooting was Pagnol's second apprenticeship: 'Korda taught me cinema'. The two worked closely together, the master of silent cinema alongside the master of theatrical speech. The resulting film was a box-office triumph.

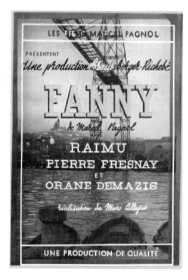

Paramount also had the screen rights to the play, *Fanny* but Kane released them, apparently believing that the success of *Marius* had exhausted the commercial potential of the Marseille comic-drama vein. In 1932, therefore, Pagnol joined forces with producer and distributor (and soon-to-be director) Roger Richebé, a fellow Marseillais, to form a company to make *Fanny* (Richebé's parents had opened one of the very first cinemas in Marseille, guaranteeing popular success – the cinema was called

Pagnol with French and Swedish Fannys (Orane Demazis and Inga Tidblad)

Le Populaire – by pledging that tickets would never cost more than a glass of beer). Pagnol adapted the play and, on Richebé's advice, gave the direction of the film to Marc Allégret, though himself participating actively in the shooting, much to Allégret's exasperation. Not that the tensions impaired the film's success, which was greater even than that of *Marius*.

In the early 1930s, Pagnol's cinematic activity went well beyond involvement in those two films. He provided scenario and dialogue for a number of films not based on his own work (including one of the first directed by Richebé, *L'Agonie des aigles*, 1933) and began his own career as a director, making films both from his adaptations of works by others (notably *Jofroi*, 1933, and *Angèle*, 1934, from stories by Provençal novelist, Jean Giono) and from his own original film scenarios (*Cigalon* and *Merlusse*, both 1935). Just prior to *César*, he directed an adaptation of his play *Topaze*, dissatisfied as he was with the 1932 Louis Gasnier version for Paramount (Pagnol's version, in which Sylvia Bataille had a role, was not much better and he withdrew the film). It was thus with some substantial directing experience that in 1936 he took on *César*. Fundamental too in these years of the move into cinema was his desire not only to make films as author–director but to do so with control over every aspect of the filmmaking process; this being the prerequisite for authorship of what would then truly be *his* films. The money earned from his plays and the first two trilogy films was used to this end and in the space of a very few years the goal was achieved: Pagnol owned his means of production.

After *Fanny*, with a group of friends and fellow dramatists, he had set up in 1933 a production and distribution company called – alluding to

United Artists – Les Auteurs Associés, which aimed to offer creative independence from the hold of the major producers. This was wound up the following year to be replaced by the Société des Films Marcel Pagnol, with Pagnol henceforth responsible to no one but himself. Along with this went the establishment of his own production facilities in Marseille: first, a small studio coupled with a processing lab, ready in 1934 in time to provide support for Renoir's *Toni*; then, with the acquisition of disaffected warehouses nearby, a substantial complex with several stages, editing and viewing rooms, and administrative offices, with the processing lab taking over the space of the initial premises; the whole set-up completed in 1938 for the shooting of Pagnol's own *La Femme du boulanger*. He also acquired cinemas in Marseille – one in 1938 was called, naturally enough, Le César (still there today).

He had guaranteed his freedom: 'I was the first in France to be free as a film-maker.' The claim is not vain: in the course of the 1930s he effectively secured the possibility of making his own films much as he pleased from start to finish. He also thereby became a serious player in the French film industry, this in the face of the resources and dominance of the capital. Marseille's distance from Paris was not unimportant in this, nor were the conditions of climate and light, nor again were the city's connections with cinema's history – the train arrived, after all, in nearby La Ciotat and a number of early Lumière films were shot in Marseille itself. The city had quickly been an important centre for film production; the Marseille-based Phocéa-Film company in particular enjoyed national success in the 1920s before ceasing activity in 1930, unable to manage the transition to sound. With its open-air studios and other facilities, the city was indeed often described (hyperbolically, but nevertheless) as 'the French Los Angeles'. Pagnol gave renewed meaning to that description and the importance of Marseille and the significance of Pagnol's studios were consolidated for a while by the German invasion of France and the city's situation in the free zone with, at first, fewer restrictions on film production.

Those who worked with Pagnol in the 1930s stress the special atmosphere of his studios; an atmosphere far from – and not just physically – that of the large Paris-based companies with the kind of hierarchical organisation that Pagnol had encountered at Paramount and which he satirised in his film *Le Schpountz* (1938). The word invariably used to characterise Pagnol's set-up by those who were directly involved is 'family' – they were, they say, members of 'la famille Pagnol' – and the impression given is of an organisation that was paternalistic, artisanal rather than industrial, out of line with standard industry practices (Renoir even talked of it as 'medieval'). Reports have it that everyone did everything and that divisions between categories of technician and between actors and technicians were never rigid (so Albert Spanna, an electrician on the set of *César*, also appears in it as the Postman). Games of bowls were an indispensable feature of the working day and everyone gathered for lunch to exchange ideas and suggestions: 'we discussed things and decided what we were going to do that afternoon', Pagnol many times recalled.

Doubtless there is truth in all this – it is hardly surprising that working in the Studios Marcel Pagnol in Marseille was a different experience from that of working in the Paramount studios in Saint-Maurice. It remains nevertheless that Pagnol was running a commercial company making commercial films for the French market. His work methods were effective not because they were pre-industrial (they were not) but because they were able to include the creation of such an atmosphere as part of the management of the production of his films. The reality was, in his words, that he was 'master in his own home', that *he* was involved in and in control of all departments of the 'familial' enterprise. He had something to which later French film-makers – Godard and Truffaut most explicitly – would look back in envy: a production situation in which nothing was out of his hands.

This independence and authority allowed him very substantial authorship of his films and Pagnol might be seen as the film-maker–author *par excellence*. His own stated conception of authorship in cinema, however, played down the film-making process and stressed writer over film-maker, denying authorship to the latter. The experience at Paramount had convinced him that for Hollywood the writer was bottom in the hierarchy of those concerned in the making of a film; whereas for him, the writer should be at the top as the very source of cinematic creation: 'it is the creation of what is going to be shot that makes one an author'. Thus Orson Welles – Pagnol's example – was the author of *Citizen Kane* when he conceived the film, not when he made it; had it been made by another director, Welles would still have been its author (for Clair, this was tantamount to claiming that Tacitus was the author of several plays by Racine). Yet even as the man-of-the-theatre Pagnol was advocating the

Shooting *César*: the confession scene (Pagnol is on the right)

writer as film-author, the man-of-the-cinema Pagnol was taking all possible steps to ensure that he would be creatively in charge of the film-making process, acknowledging *that* as the condition and guarantee of his authorship. Welles himself, speaking a few years after the war, is helpful here: 'I think that today the importance of the director in film-making is exaggerated, while the writer hardly ever gets the place of honour due to him. To me people like Marcel Pagnol ... mean more than any others in the French cinema. In my opinion, the writer should have the first and last word in film-making, the only better alternative being the writer–director, but with the stress on the first word.' The terms fit Pagnol's practice: it is as 'writer–director' that he strove to exist in cinema.

All of this, it must be stressed again, is in the context of the opportunity now offered for the development of a cinema of speech, this determining Pagnol's commitment to cinema. Needless to say, everything to do with sound in film became of passionate practical interest and it is only typical that he should at one point have had Philips come up with a special sound system for his company. As it is typical too that the writer–director Pagnol should have spent most of the time during the shooting of a film with the sound engineer, always regarding the quality of the dialogue as the key to the film's making.

Doctrine

When *The Jazz Singer* came to France in 1929, only two cinemas were equipped to show it: one in Paris and Richebé's Capitole in Marseille. In France as elsewhere, the advent of talking pictures had considerable economic and artistic repercussions. Bringing with them the barriers of national languages, they were a boost for what was, at the end of the 1920s, a French film industry in financial crisis; at the same time, however, France was far behind in the development of sound technology and dependent on costly American and German licences for the systems with which to equip studios and cinemas. The advantage of the language barrier, moreover, was short-lived: American Paramount and German Tobis-Klangfilm could produce French-language films in their studios outside Paris and the development of dubbing rapidly put paid to the language-barrier problem. Nevertheless, national demand for films in French with French subjects was strong and production by those French companies able to manage the switch to sound greatly increased, dominated by that of two large consortia, Gaumont-Franco-Film-Aubert and Pathé-Natan, though both were financially precarious and bankrupt by the late 1930s.

Concern regarding the threat to national production posed by the level of financial investment required for sound and the foreseen increase in the power of Hollywood was accompanied in France as elsewhere by forcefully voiced defences of *cinema*, of its *art* as a matter of images. The introduction of synchronised speech, it was contended, could only result in a hybrid medium that would negate the aesthetic achievement of the silent cinema, leading to a cinematically impoverished 'theatrical cinema'. Debates as to how sound should be used and arguments against its use at all were rife.

It is into those debates and arguments that the cinematic newcomer Pagnol entered with his 1930 *Journal* article. The ideas sketched out there were then elaborated in several pieces written during the years he was turning himself into a film-maker. True to character, he had to have his own publication in which to promulgate these ideas and so founded a review, *Les Cahiers du film*. Based in Marseille, it brought out four issues from December 1933 to September 1934 (there was perhaps a fifth, in November, but direct evidence of it has proved elusive). Reactions to these ideas were fiery and Pagnol, rather theatrically, talked of the *Cahiers* as having 'unleashed a long, fiercely raging brawl around the corpse of silent cinema'. The review's aim was the presentation of 'cinematographic doctrine' (its subtitle was *Revue de doctrine cinématographique*), meaning *Pagnol's* doctrine as expressed in a series of articles under the overall title 'Cinématurgie de Paris' (*cinématurgie* was an ambitious allusion to

Lessing's treatise on dramatic composition, the *Hamburgische Dramaturgie*). These articles apart, the review consisted largely of pieces about Pagnol's films and productions; indeed a second series of the review, from January 1941 until January 1944, abandoned doctrine and, while styling itself 'the French review of French cinema', was pretty much a fan magazine, devoted more or less exclusively to news and photos of Pagnol and his films, studios and actors.

Pagnol's views were decided and decidedly expressed: the silent film was handicapped but had been able to draw strength from its handicap (for example, by reaching across the boundaries of national languages); that strength can be acknowledged but silent cinema is finished: the need is to recognise what a fully abled cinema can do. Hence, and facing hostility from both writers (the talking picture regarded as travesty and competitor of the theatre) and film-makers (spoken language regarded as endangering the art of images), Pagnol develops his doctrine to meet that need, aiming at nothing less than 'a theory and practice of the talking film'. Not that the 'theory' produced was other than itself emphatically simple: the silent film must go; the talking film must talk; the talking film is only a means of expression, 'not of creation'. The difference between silent and talking cinema is absolute; the latter is not to be seen as merely an improvement of the former, as though it were just a matter of adding on speech. Lament for the silent cinema, attempts to carry its forms of achievement into the cinema of the talking film are misguided. The new cinema is precisely *new* and must be *newly* conceived, its true potential realised. As to what that meant, Pagnol's views were provocative: cinema's potential lay in its service to dramatic art, 'the only noble art'; in itself, it is at most a minor art and Pagnol can happily declare that *as a film-maker* he has no art – 'none at all: I do cinema' (this fits too with his idea, as distinct from his practice, of authorship). Dramatic art to which cinema owes allegiance, is 'the art of recounting actions and expressing feelings by means of characters who act and speak'. Given this, there are clear rules and principles: the image is a support for the text, changes of shot must be determined by and useful for the dramatic action, and so on.

Naturally, all this could only exacerbate the attacks on Pagnol as seeking to subordinate cinema to theatre, as the apologist of canned theatre. Many of his oft repeated declarations seemed to confirm this: what else after all could be meant by assertions such as 'the talking film is the art of recording, fixing and broadcasting theatre'? At the same time, however, he would declare theatre itself to be only a minor art, just one of the arts through which drama can be expressed and now overtaken by cinema. It is a matter not simply of bringing plays to the screen but of 'reinventing theatre', the possibility of such a reinvention being cinema's gift to the dramatist: 'the talking film is a higher form of theatre because in the cinema the author has a complete freedom'. No more theatrical constraints, no more artificially staged entries and exits, no more cumbersome scene changes, no more need for lengthy explanations of who the characters are when this can be easily shown, no more problems of what the audience in different parts of the auditorium will be able to see now that the spectator's vision can be focused on this or that close-up detail on the large luminous screen. Pagnol's doctrine, in fact, is not about collapsing cinema into theatre but about developing cinema as an original mode of dramatic representation. That is what counts, not theatrical form, and a film that transposed a play to the screen without filmically reconceiving it would be 'a bad talking film'. Pagnol thus firmly distinguishes himself from the other highly successful dramatist of 1930s' French cinema, Sacha Guitry: 'Guitry is photographic theatre ... the camera set in the prompt box.' It remains, however, that Pagnol's doctrinal formulations sometimes come close to suggesting 'filmed theatre' and that aspects of his trilogy films themselves may at times seem to warrant that description.

2

. . . .

THE MARSEILLE TRILOGY: SYNOPSES

'Marius'

Marius works in the Vieux-Port bar owned by his father, César, but yearns to set sail for distant lands on one of the ships that visit the port. He is loved by and loves Fanny who sells shellfish on a stall, owned by her mother, Honorine, just outside the bar. A place he is offered on a ship falls through and he and Fanny become lovers. A few weeks later, the opportunity of another place presents itself, on the *Malaisie*, a great three-master. Fanny, realising the strength of his yearning and despite the pain his departure will cause her, leads him to believe that she will marry Panisse, a well-off master sail-maker, recently widowed and much older than her, who has his business on the Vieux-Port. Marius allows himself to be convinced and the film ends with Fanny fainting into César's arms as the *Malaisie* sets sail. César, whose roughness towards Marius conceals the strength of his love for him, is unaware of his son's departure.

'Fanny'

The film begins where *Marius* ended, with César carrying the unconscious Fanny to her mother's house where he and Honorine learn of Marius's departure. Devastated and outwardly disowning his son, César longs for news of him and finally receives a letter that has little in it to comfort Fanny who now discovers she is two months pregnant. Honorine insists she marry Panisse who has renewed his suit and who accepts her even after she has informed him of her pregnancy. Indeed, the childless Panisse is overjoyed at this 'gift' of a child, hoping for the son he has always wanted and who will enable his business to become 'Panisse & Fils'. César brutally opposes the marriage which he sees as depriving him of his future grandson but is brought to accept it as for the best; Fanny duly gives birth to a son, Césariot. Fifteen months or so later, Marius returns unexpectedly on a brief mission from his ship, learns of the birth, guesses the child is his and urges Fanny, still deeply in love with him, to leave Panisse. César persuades him that Césariot's future would be more secure with Panisse as his father and leads him away, leaving Fanny stricken with grief.

Marius: Marius dreams of the sea, Fanny of him

Fanny: Fanny, pregnant, goes to pray to the Virgin at Notre-Dame de la Garde

César: Marius and Fanny acknowledge their continuing love

César informs Elzéar that Panisse is dying

The confession scene begins

Panisse's dining room: Claudine, Honorine, M.Brun, the Chauffeur, César, Escartefigue, the altar boy

Césariot arrives from Paris in his Polytechnique uniform

Fanny and Panisse refuse Elzéar's demand that Césariot be told the truth

Marius listens as Fernand reads the
notice of Panisse's death

Césariot leads his father's funeral procession

Fanny's tears as she names Marius
as Césariot's father

Césariot gives vent to his feelings on learning he is
Marius's son

Honorine watches Césariot's boat
depart for Toulon…

… and Fanny gives him short shrift on his return

Fanny affirms her rights as a woman …

… and remembers the pleasure she had with Marius

Marius returns to the bar after years of absence for the great scene of family drama

Marius leaves the bar …

… and arrives for the next and final scene of his reconciliation with Fanny

'César'

Twenty years have elapsed: Césariot is about to graduate brilliantly from the École Polytechnique in Paris; Fanny now plays a major part in running Panisse's expanding business; Panisse is dying and the film opens with César summoning the priest to minister to him. Panisse makes his confession in front of his friends and is then privately urged by the priest to tell Césariot the truth about his paternity, something known to everyone but him; this Panisse refuses to do and dies soon after. The evening following the funeral, Fanny reveals the truth to Césariot who reacts with bitterness. He decides to find out what his father is like and, deceiving Fanny into believing he is visiting a Polytechnicien friend, visits Marius incognito in Toulon where the latter now owns a garage. Marius's associate, as a joke, convinces Césariot that Marius is involved in crime but subsequently acknowledges this to be untrue. Césariot reveals to Marius, who is in Marseille on business, that he is his son. A great scene of recrimination and explanation takes place between the main protagonists – Marius, Fanny, César, Césariot – and Marius leaves, telling Césariot that if ever he wants to see his father again he knows where to find him. The next and final scene takes place in the country where Marius and Fanny have agreed to meet. Despite their love, Marius insists that he cannot marry her because of her social situation since it would be thought he was doing so for her – for Panisse's – money. He says goodbye and goes back to his car. César, unseen, has listened to their conversation and takes Fanny to Marius who is unable to start the car (César has removed a vital part). César informs the couple that Césariot accepts that his mother and father should marry. He leaves them and the film ends with Fanny and Marius walking off together down a country lane.

3

....

'CÉSAR'

Film and Play

Pagnol had intended to write *César* as a play. A contract with the actor Raimu made in 1935 indicates the latter's agreement to play 'the role of César (stage play)'. Pagnol, however, changed his mind: unlike *Marius* and *Fanny*, César would be written directly for the screen. The change was influenced by the difficulties in assembling the actors from the first two films for the duration of the run of a play and those actors *were* the characters they had created; it was unthinkable that audiences would accept substitutes. Easier by far was to get them together for the shorter period of the making of a film. This practical consideration went along with Pagnol's shift of interest to cinema, now become his major area of activity and one in which he had already achieved success as a director. To write and make *César* as a film was a natural step.

Shooting began early in May 1936 and the film had its 'gala night' opening at Pagnol's Noailles cinema in Marseille on 19 September 1936, with its general public release the following day. *César* the play was not completed until after the war, receiving its premiere on 14 December 1946 at the Théâtre des Variétés in Paris. Raimu had died in September of that year and the role of César on stage in this final movement of the trilogy was thus never his (it was taken by Henri Vilbert, later to play the priest in Pagnol's *Manon des sources*, 1952). The play did not do well, its lack of success seeming to justify Pagnol's reluctance to have the play performed while the film *César* was still showing.

There are a number of versions of *César*, taking film, published film scenarios and play together, and the differences between them are often substantial – indeed *César* is something of a nightmare in this respect. If the play retains large parts of the film's dialogue, it nevertheless differs quite considerably, which must have surprised and disappointed those in the audience in 1946 who had seen the film (almost everyone): bits of dialogue are taken from one character and given to another, characters are presented slightly differently, new elements are added (including a policeman who comes on several times for a laborious piece of comic play) and major – and hugely popular – scenes disappear (notably, the card game after Panisse's funeral, his place at the table pathetically empty).

The first published text of *César* appeared in 1937, not long after the film. With an introductory note by Pagnol lauding the freedom afforded the dramatist by the talking film, this to a large extent reproduces the film's dialogue and describes its settings as though it were the text of a play. It was succeeded in 1967 by a revised version for an edition of Pagnol's *Oeuvres complètes*; described as 'film made in 1936', this differs in many respects from the 1937 version and is the version currently available. Leaving aside the variations between the printed versions, the film itself is frustratingly hard to pin down, with filmographies showing indications of length alone that range from 117 to more than 170 minutes. All that need be said here is that there are basically two differently edited versions: one of around 170 minutes, the other of around 135. The first, longer version, of which a copy is held by the Cinémathèque in Toulouse, is doubtless the one initially released (critics at the time variously noted the film's length as between two hours fifty minutes and three hours). The shorter version, shorter by twenty minutes or so, probably dates from just after the war and from then on has been the version familiar to audiences.

The shorter version, however, is not merely a truncated replica of the longer one. If it lacks scenes present in the latter, it also has scenes absent from it, scenes nevertheless shot during the making of the film in 1936; the most startling example being that of the great – now classic – scene of the dying Panisse's confession (a scene included, however, in the 1937 published text of the film!). The longer version is longer particularly in the later part of the film after Panisse's death. Among the scenes not in the shorter version is one featuring a virtuoso performance by Raimu in which César questions his friends as to whether or not he is of a choleric nature (confusion surrounds even this one scene, which I heard described by Pierre Tchernia – France's Mr Cinema – in a television programme devoted to Pagnol as 'hitherto unseen'). To cap it all, the 1937 published text contains material from both film versions and some from neither!

In what follows, it is the shorter version that will be taken as the film of reference, with mention of the longer one where necessary. Apart from being better than the longer one, this is the version known for almost all of the film's existence – enjoyed and loved. (The British National Film Archive copy of *César* matches neither the longer nor the shorter versions described above and, with a running time of just under two hours, appears to be considerably cut version of the former.)

The Troupe

'Ah! I had a wonderful troupe!' Pagnol exclaimed, looking back on his films of the 1930s. Indeed he did, and this is important for *César*, as for Pagnol's cinema overall. To think of the characters of *César* and the trilogy is to think at once of the *company* of actors, the company we keep across the films – so many familiar faces, voices, gestures. What Pagnol had is no longer possible, Godard was later to regret: 'the phenomenon of the troupe, of the family to which spectators are responsive' ('family' again). The cinematic reinvention of theatre for Pagnol was first and foremost a matter of working with actors. He drew around him a group of actors who come and go from film to film, sustaining a Pagnolesque style and vision of cinema. Nowhere is this more so than in the trilogy where the main roles are played by the same actors throughout (with the exception of Escartefigue, played by a different actor in *Fanny* for reasons of availability). Nine actors appear in all three films and almost all of the actors who appear in *César* turn up – the fact of the troupe – in other Pagnol films of the 30s.

Cinema historians Raymond Chirat and Olivier Barrot talk of 'the excentrics of French cinema': 'These are the second roles, supporting actors, as necessary for the evocative power of films as the stars. Active members of the family of players, catalysts of our complicity, these "excentrics" (excentricity: "state of being far from the centre"...) are our friends'. It is this kind of 'friendship' that Pagnol creates. Most of his actors are just such excentrics and in fact become so as a result of his films. When members of the troupe appear in films not by Pagnol, they carry over with them their recognition – their familiarity – as his actors. Even an actor such

The troupe, soon back on your screens

as Fernand Charpin, who has numerous other film roles, always also appears *coming from* Pagnol (indeed, in Renoir's *Chotard et Cie*, 1933, just after *Marius* and *Fanny*, it is as though we have Charpin–Panisse back on the screen before us).

The trilogy films and Pagnol's 30s films generally might be seen in many ways as films of second roles. Of course, there are leading roles with leading actors but then perhaps it is not quite as simple as 'of course'. Clearly, Pierre Fresnay was a star of stage and silent screen and, unlike the others, his collaboration with Pagnol was confined to the trilogy alone: he created the role of Marius and it was identified with him but he remained separate from it, beyond Pagnol. Orane Demazis, however, gained her status from her role as Fanny and almost her entire film career in the 30s was with Pagnol. Raimu, well known in the theatre, found real fame as César in *Marius*, and some of his finest roles thereafter were in Pagnol films; though hardly a second-role excentric, he has something all the same of the excentric's catalysing familiarity and his performance as César stays with him always.

The actors were Pagnol's raw materials, to be fashioned into film characters whose reality as such was filled with and determined by the particular screen presence of their actors. To say which might have annoyed Pagnol who held that one of cinema's advantages over the theatre was its capacity to 'suppress the reality of the actor': since the flesh-and-blood actor was not physically present in the cinema, his or her physical and mental individuality could be eliminated in the interests of the pure character (he deplored the need to include the actors' names in the credits). The trilogy hardly confirms this: yes, the actors become the characters but the characters emerge from *and fit* the actors. There is a constant, excessive overlapping in which we see character *and* performance both: Raimu *is* César but the character César *is* the actor Raimu, is made of all the emphatic gestural and vocal weight of Raimu himself, his massive *thereness*.

Performance is all-important, fundamental for the particular mesh of theatre and cinema – the theatrical-cinematic mode – that Pagnol largely invents. Nothing like Guitry's theatre-on-screen, his cinema is about the theatricalisation of film, the achievement of a style of film performance that depends not just on the acting *in* the film but equally on the acting *of* the film, the way in which the film cinematically materialises its actors. For this, in these first years of the talkies, it was not unimportant that most of Pagnol's troupe had little or no previous film experience. Again, this includes the three leading actors, of whom Fresnay alone had had any such experience; Raimu had been in a couple of silents but his cinema career only really began in the year of *Marius*, while Fanny was Demazis's first film role. Most of the troupe had a music-hall background, bringing with them a performance style that pulled away from the conventions of the classic stage towards a variety theatre of heightened humours and enlarged emotions. The Parisian, conservatoire-trained Fresnay, once more the exception, had to adapt to this style and the result can be seen in *César* in the emphatic posturings and gesturings of the scene near the end when Marius confronts César and Fanny and the family drama plays itself out. There is something in Pagnol's films of the bodily expressiveness of the silent cinema, as though the cinematic reinvention of theatre needed to avoid the trap of a cinema tailored to an accepted polish of acting. Marseille was crucial here, its own excentricity – the distance of its culture from that of the capital – offering Pagnol a certain line of innovation.

Film performance in Pagnol is immediately a performance of, in, with and around language (no surprise that he sat with the sound engineer). André Bazin described him as 'one of the greatest authors of *talking* films; if not the greatest, at any rate something like their "genius"'; adding, this was in 1958, that he was the only director since 1930 to have dared 'a verbal excessiveness comparable with that [sic] of the Griffithses and Stroheims of the age of the silent image'. If actors are the raw materials of the films, language is their foundation, language as speech and actors as *characters in speech*, unstoppably bound to a course and style of language. Pagnol, that is, *films* speech, which is not a matter of reproducing a text (despite his talk at times of recording theatre) but of having us *see* speech: speech in action in the image, working in the film (to Gilles Deleuze's categories of image-movement and image-time, we could add that of image-speech, the exploration of which might place Pagnol in a surprisingly modern perspective). The characters, like us, live in and through their speech and it is the fact of that 'living through' which is filmed in *César* and the trilogy, to give a representation – precisely a *talking picture* – of how speech performs. Marseille was crucial here too in its off-centredness from dominant standards of speech and accent: Marseille as the trilogy's linguistic substance, its exaggeration of language into film.

The Trilogy

Pagnol maintained that he began the trilogy intending that Fanny and Marius would marry. Perhaps, though there is no particular evidence – and

Fanny swoons at the end of
Marius ...

... and grieves at the end of
Fanny

some to the contrary – that from the start he even envisaged a *trilogy*.
Certainly, an ending that brought Fanny and Marius together accorded
with his idea of the resolution required by comedy. If the preceding films
had been richly comic, their endings had been abrupt, painfully
*un*resolved: the last shot of *Marius* has Fanny fainting and César calling for
his son, pitifully ignorant of the latter's departure; the last shot of *Fanny*
has Fanny against the panelling of her dining room, convulsed with grief
after Marius has once again left for the sea, this time at César's own behest.

César follows on from there; not immediately, as *Fanny* does from
Marius, picking up from the moment of Fanny's fainting, but twenty or
so years later. It opens with César leaving Panisse's establishment on the
Vieux-Port and making his way up to the Basilique Saint-Victor; a

cinematic trajectory that matches Fanny's journey across the city in *Fanny* when, her pregnancy confirmed, she leaves the Doctor's and climbs to Notre-Dame de la Garde to beg help from the Virgin. César's mission is to fetch the priest to administer the last rites to Panisse, Fanny's husband, whose dying moments are this film's beginning. In the years since *Fanny*, the love child of Fanny and Marius has been brought up as Panisse's son and is now a brilliant student at the prestigious École Polytechnique in Paris. The death of her husband will free Fanny but will also bring the revelation to Césariot that Panisse was not his father, a revelation which triggers the drama of the film.

Like the first two films, *César* is set in the Vieux-Port but opens out a little more, with some scenes taking place beyond the confines of the port and, indeed, outside Marseille itself. The imagination of the sea, however, has gone; there are none of the emphatic close-ups of sails and masts so powerful in *Marius*; and Marius, who dreamed of great sailing ships and distant islands, is found lying on the floor repairing motorcars in his garage in Toulon. Time has moved on: there is a new, third generation, embodied by Césariot, whose horizons are not bound by Marseille and whose social aspirations are far from those of the bar owner and his son. But then, it is the same family drama, to be resolved within much the same, seemingly unchanged, little Vieux-Port world, with most of the action again taking place in César's bar or Panisse and Fanny's shop.

César is the head of the family, the central figure. After *Marius* and *Fanny*, the final part of the trilogy is called after him, the title going generationally backwards not forwards (*César*, not *Césariot*). César had

Césariot and Marius, his unsuspecting father, fishing near Toulon

dominated from the start, as Raimu had intended he would when he refused the role of Panisse originally offered him and insisted on playing what Pagnol had envisaged as only a 'second role'. Physically, César towers over everyone; dramatically, he rules over the films. Pagnol saw him as 'a great sympathetic brute'; which is what we see, save that the sympathetic side is not always apparent. The trilogy opens with him reprimanding Marius and shouting at Fanny to get back to her shellfish stall; it ends with him violently shaking Marius and ordering him to remain with Fanny (this last outburst is sympathetic in its motivation – he wants them to agree to marry – but too reminiscent of the brutality we have seen before). For most of the trilogy, he regards Marius, in his twenties when it begins, much as a hopeless child, deserving of scorn and correction (he is sarcastically astounded when M. Brun in *Fanny* calls Marius 'a young *man*').

The key word that attaches to César throughout the trilogy is *coléreux*: he is irascible, given to fits of anger that reinforce his dominating presence: 'he isn't nasty but he shouts a lot', comments Marius early on. In the scene cut from *César* mentioned above, César demands his friends' opinion as to whether he could be regarded as choleric; when they remain nervously silent, he provides the answer himself by launching into an angry tirade on the injustice of such an idea (ironically, in *César* he of all people declares Fanny to be *coléreuse*). Behind the irritability and general brusqueness of manner lies a love for Marius that *pudeur* – his sense of fatherly reserve – prevents him from showing (unless precisely in bearish grumblings and bursts of anger). His son's unannounced departure – had it been announced, he would have forbidden it – is experienced as a betrayal involving such depths of emotional hurt that he refuses thereafter to speak of him. We learn, moreover, that some time between *Fanny* and

César choleric at the trilogy's beginning ...   ... and end

César, a violent altercation led to blows between father and son, bringing communication between them to an end.

The trilogy starts with Marius and the contradiction between his love for Fanny and his wish to leave. He is for ever gazing out to sea and reciting the names and destinations of departing ships, in thrall to his *envie d'ailleurs*, his desire for *elsewhere*: for the Iles Sous-le-Vent – the Leeward Islands – of which he once heard sailors speak and which gave a name to his desire. Reality, however, drained the romance and after a while, he tells us in *César*, he had had enough of the sea. Like his father, if differently, he is not always sympathetic. In *Marius*, he self-servingly goes along with Fanny's pretence that she might well marry Panisse and thinks that he should go off to sea; while in *Fanny*, he angrily asserts a right to her and her son and demands that she leave Panisse. This unattractiveness is heightened by an occasional tendency to a somewhat aggressively snivelling self-pity and by Fresnay's acting which can fall into an abruptness of gesture and a setness of expression that harden the Marius he portrays.

Fanny in the first film of the trilogy overlays her love for Marius with an occasional coquettishness, trying to kindle his jealousy and make him declare his feelings for her by flirting with Panisse. In *Fanny*, she is focus of the film and we find her broken-hearted at Marius's departure. Pregnant, her wish is to stay single and raise the child on her own. Persuaded that marriage to Panisse is best, she refuses to marry without telling him of the pregnancy. When Marius unexpectedly reappears in the middle of the night, she strives to resist him but comes close to yielding before César arrives to save the situation.

Along with these three eponymous characters, the other major figure in the drama is Panisse, as physically round as César is imposingly large. Ridiculed at first for his wish to marry the much younger Fanny, he good-naturedly accepts her initial refusal and her love for Marius (at the end of *Marius*, aware of Fanny's distress, he tries desperately to warn César of his son's imminent departure). Told she is pregnant, he is quick to accept her, overjoyed at the thought of a son (no one envisages Fanny might have a girl), and proves – as everyone insists – a generous husband and a devoted father. We learn too in *César* that his generosity extended to secretly helping Marius to arange a loan for his garage.

Around these four main characters cluster the members of an 'extended family', the Vieux-Port group, who have mostly known each other since childhood. The sole outsider – but part of the group nevertheless – is M. Brun, a Lyonnais among the Marseillais (he uses the more formal *vous* mode of address to the others, as they do to him). Most of these characters are there in the trilogy from the beginning, with one or two of them coming in later as the action requires; Fanny's Aunt Claudine and the Doctor make their appearance in the second film when Fanny's pregnancy and social predicament become the focus. Some have bigger parts in this or that film: Honorine, Fanny's mother, has important scenes in *Marius* and is well to the fore in *Fanny* but less prominent in *César*; the Chauffeur has a larger part in *César* than in the previous films where he is often really no more than the occasional butt of César's ire and irony. Central throughout is César's bar, where the regulars group themselves around its owner. Individually, Panisse, Escartefigue, M. Brun and the Chauffeur come with their characteristic attitudes and expressions, comic in themselves and the cause of comedy in others. Together, joined at times in *César* by the Doctor, they form something of a chorus, commenting on and responding to events.

The characters cross three generations: the first that of César and Panisse, along with Honorine, Claudine, Escartefigue, the priest Elzéar, Dr Venelle and the Chauffeur (notwithstanding small differences in age); the second that of Marius and Fanny; the third that of Césariot (M. Brun is described by Pagnol as 'young' but his manner and his place in the bar group make him generationally a little uncertain, older than his probable years). There is a notable falling off as we move down the generations, with Césariot standing alone in the third (Dromart, his Polytechnique friend appears only briefly). The weight of the trilogy is with the older generation; the melodrama with the second; the future with the third. Except that no such future is presented: Césariot is wooden and stiffly lifeless (André Fouché's flatly prim acting is no help and serves only to exacerbate Césariot's separation from the life of the others) and is given no place in the ending which centres on Marius and Fanny *and César*, still as emphatically there at the end as he was at the beginning. Things have changed and will change, yet not so much: Marius and Fanny, after all, are going back to the Vieux-Port and will carry on Panisse's business. César alludes to them having children but anchors this to the past, to the preservation of his name.

The characters can be distinguished in terms of social position. Going roughly upwards, we have: the Chauffeur, so called because of his employment as stoker for the steam-driven Vieux-Port ferry, though in *César* he seems to be at the service of Fanny and Césariot; Escartefigue, captain of the ferry-boat ('master on board after God'); Honorine, who sells her fish from a quayside stall, as well as owning the stall where Fanny sells her mussels and clams; César, proprietor of a bar handed down from his great-grandfather (a slave-trader); the more educated M. Brun, a customs inspector; Dr Venelle with his city practice; Panisse, from a well-off family and owner of an increasingly prosperous business. As for Marius and Fanny, they work for their father and mother respectively, with the former subsequently becoming part-owner of a modest garage and the latter marrying into Panisse's wealth and eventually owning his business (at the end of *César*, Marius has misgivings about marrying her given the difference now between them in wealth and social position). Social and class differences, however, are smoothed over in this Vieux-Port world: Panisse, César, Escartefigue, M. Brun, the Chauffeur, even the Doctor, form an easy group in the bar, talking, joking, playing cards. Where differences gain significance is in the dramatic action, as Fanny marries Panisse and Césariot moves into a completely different – and Parisian – social milieu. Yet even then, Césariot apart, these class-different characters are close knit within a little community dependent on a shared culture of the past, an environment in which they keep at bay the threat of divisions, even while such divisions become, in *César* especially, fundamental to the characters' reactions and responses to the drama in which they are involved.

The marital status of the characters is significant. César, Panisse, Honorine and Claudine are widowed; Escartefigue, M. Brun, the Chauffeur and the Doctor are single as far at least as we see them in the trilogy; a passing remark suggests M. Brun might be married; Escartefigue is certainly married

Fanny and Césariot: dress and décor as class representation

and his wife appears marginally in *Fanny* but has whatever substance she has in the films only as the subject of a running joke about him being cuckolded; the Chauffeur is single for all we know, though seen happy in *César* in the arms of a chambermaid. There are, in other words, no *couples*, save the broken one of Marius and Fanny and the reparative one of her and Panisse which, after Césariot is born, gives the trilogy its only version of a standard nuclear family. Not that anything is seen of that family until Fanny is herself about to be widowed (the family years are elided in the lapse of time between *Fanny* and *César*) and it is anyway problematic: a family in which the child is not the father's and the mother's desire belongs to someone else (both Panisse and Fanny are explicit on their marriage's lack of sexual passion).

Marius and Fanny begin the trilogy in a situation of homology: he has a father but no mother (César: 'I was his mother'); she has a mother but no father. Honorine is to Fanny as César is to Marius and in the same strongly possessive way that César loves his son, Honorine loves her daughter. Like him, she shifts from love to anger as the explosive expression of that love. Learning in *Fanny* of her daughter's pregnancy, she seesaws between paroxysms of rage and bouts of hysterical anxiety whenever Fanny swoons, reverting to rage the moment she regains consciousness (Claudine: 'As soon as she faints you cry, and as soon as she recovers you start again'). As César runs a bar, so Honorine has her fish stall and, as he with his son, so she with her daughter is commandingly assertive, ever ready to lay down the family law (Fanny *must* marry Panisse).

The chronology of the trilogy's unfolding is reasonably clear. When it opens, César, Panisse and Escartefigue are in their early fifties, Fanny is eighteen and Marius is twenty. The beginning of *Fanny* is exactly contemporary with the end of *Marius* and the film then moves forward to the birth of Césariot seven months later ('a seven-month baby', Panisse insists, wanting to hide the fact of its conception with Marius nine months earlier) and then forward again eight months or so to Marius's return and his attempt to claim Fanny and the child. Between *Fanny* and *César*, twenty-odd years have passed and the 'seven-month baby' is now roughly the same age as Fanny when the trilogy started. Marius and Fanny have gained in independence: he is his own master in his own business; she is married with a grown-up son and herself manages a substantial business (and acts and dresses accordingly, even driving an expensive car).

Two decades have elapsed but the relation of trilogy time to historical time is vague: in what period(s) are the events of the trilogy set? If *Marius* were set in 1931, the year of its making, then, realistically, *César* would be set futuristically in the early 1950s, which it is not. Likewise, if *César* were set in 1936, the year it was made, then *Marius* would be set at the time of World War I, which it is not (the war is barely referred to in the trilogy films and plays; in *César*, the Chauffeur says he was thirteen at the time and Panisse mentions service at Verdun). All of this points to the world of the trilogy as being *in and out of* time. Changing times are *softly* acknowledged (by *César*, for example, Panisse's business is with motors rather than sails) but period specification is uncertain: the Vieux-Port stays much the same and the period remains indistinct, just some time in an elastic mid-1920s that can contain all the trilogy's twenty or so years. The trilogy, in other words, is historically static: what change takes place does so within the family and turns round again in the end to the beginning, comes back to the Marius–Fanny–César grouping of the opening scene. There is a sense of a time out of time, of a world set apart in which the characters move along without much interaction with outside reality. The bar, supposedly in the heart of Marseille, in an area busy with people, is sunk in a kind of slumber; indeed, it is empty of customers, frequented only by the same three or four friends of the owner.

The period of the making of *César*, from May to September 1936, coincided with the coming to power of the Front Populaire. This left-wing coalition – it included socialist, radical and communist parties – was elected on a programme of wide-ranging social, economic and political reforms and saw its purpose in government as that of, in the words of its leader Léon Blum, 'seeing if, through action accomplished within the existing regime, it is possible to prepare in minds and things the inevitable advent of the [socialist] regime which remains our strength and our aim'. Workers' confidence in the new political situation gave rise to a spontaneous outbreak of strikes voicing demands which had previously seemed impossible and Blum's government quickly brought in a number of measures with direct effect on people's lives; notably, the institution of paid holidays and the forty-hour working week. The euphoria of the first months, however, was short-lived. Destabilised by the strikes, ironically enough the expression of the hopes it had raised, the Front came up against an economic crisis that devaluation in September 1936 failed to resolve, at the same time that the growing threat of war forced it into a costly programme of rearmament. The coalition, moreover, was increasingly precarious, with sharp policy divergences amongst its component parties, and the government was eventually defeated on a motion concerning the control of finances, resulting in Blum's resignation in June 1937. After this, the Front dragged lamely on until the fall of a second Blum government in April of the following year.

Nothing of the social and political crisis that led to the formation of the Front, nothing of the excitement of its first months in government enters *César*. One thing might be noted however: the films of the trilogy precede paid holidays; Pagnol's Marseille is brought to a national public for most of whom that city and the Midi generally are, so far as direct knowledge is concerned, pretty much *terrae incognitae*. Pagnol, that is, *gives* people Marseille – something to which we will return.

Values

Pagnol's literary advice to his *Fortunio* friends was simple: 'let us be classical, clear and moderate'. The young Pagnol was hostile to modern literary experimentation and above all to that represented by the work of the influential André Gide, the 'crucial contemporary' as he had come to be regarded (ironically Gide, who was in a relationship with Marc Allégret, turned up on the Vieux-Port to watch the shooting of exterior scenes for *Fanny*). The advice is expressive of Pagnol's attitudes overall. Reason and lower middle-class 'common sense' merge in a vision of things that stays largely within accepted terms. Whatever culturally partakes of modernity is kept within the range of a set of conventional assumptions and values: Fanny turns into something of a new woman but the old story has her in its frame and the paternal, patriarchal César walks off at the end having achieved a proper conclusion. Paris is as far off and alien in *César* as it had been in *Marius* and distance from one's local community is a displacement from true identity. The trilogy world, that is, exists in the *present past*: something of the actuality of the modern can be felt but the past contains it. Not that the past is seen as ideal – the generation of Marius and Fanny suffers from it – but it is nevertheless in essential ways better – even if, again, its treatment of Fanny is questioned. Significantly, the younger generation, limited to Césariot, is accorded scant importance, while the actual present of this 1936 film remains off-screen, has no place in the world which the trilogy creates and reworks.

The importance of the local, César, over the Parisian, Césariot, for the centring of the film's values is epitomised by the exchange between them when the latter discovers Marius is his father. César's reply to Césariot's bitterness at finding he stems from a line of bar-owners is cutting: 'education may have embellished your brain but it's spoilt your heart'. In the 1946 play, Pagnol stressed the class terms of this: César recalls how Césariot had been ashamed to acknowledge him as his godfather in front of a friend whose father owned forty cafés in Paris 'If his father has forty bistros, then he's forty times more bistro than me ... Oh! I know there's a big difference. The young man's father is better than me. What gives his work its real class is that he gets it done by others ... my work, *I* do it, as my father did it, and his father, and as you would have, if your father hadn't been a navigating madman.' The film's sympathy lies here with César but what he expresses is not so much social criticism as a petit-bourgeois distrust of Paris, success, wealth, bourgeois ease. All of which, of course, were by then possessed by Pagnol, he who could not wait to get to Paris but who, wealthy and famous, returns to Marseille and projects in his films a world to which he and their audience can belong, which they can consensually *enjoy*. The films' reality is that of a populist cinema which eschews politics, knows little authority beyond the family and roots itself in 'the local'. Again, this is not simple. The values, even if confirmed, do not go without contradiction: César dominates but this is often shown as destructive and the films – and Pagnol through the films – in no way align themselves merely with him. Fanny's standing up to him and for herself in much of *César* has its own value here (it is the independence she shows in this that prompts César to declare her *coléreuse*).

Along with which, there is much in Pagnol of a certain 'radical-socialist' tradition: sceptical of established conventions and hierarchies and wedded to the defence of a social order of equality and merit against extremes of left or right. This is the tradition embodied in the figure of the *instituteur* so familiar to Pagnol; as well as his father, two aunts and an uncle were *instituteurs*, products of the system of public education created by education minister, Jules Ferry at the beginning of the 1880s. Ferry's aim was to provide lay schooling in towns and villages across France, with primary education obligatory for boys and girls between the ages of six and thirteen. Écoles Normales were established nationwide to train the *instituteurs*, and *institutrices*, drawn from modest backgrounds, who were to be responsible for this 'public instruction'. *Laïcité* –

secularism, the separation of state from Church – was fundamental: the instruction provided was to accord with republican values, in opposition to clericalism and conservatism and to embody a social vision of the betterment of the people; this exemplified indeed by the personal betterment achieved by the *instituteurs* themselves. In *La Gloire de mon père*, Pagnol remembered his father's 'socio-political lectures' on the future society 'in which châteaux would become hospitals'. The battle for *laïcité* against obscurantist and reactionary forces was social-political and seen as vital for the safeguard and development of the republic (as I write, the need to defend *laïcité* against the encroachments of religion is again being strongly asserted with regard to the so-called 'Islamic headscarf' and legislation has been introduced to forbid the wearing of 'ostensible religious signs' in schools and other public institutions).

The figure and values of the *instituteur* are strongly present in Pagnol's work. In *La Femme du boulanger*, *instituteur* and priest stand opposed, with the former carrying the day (there is even a scene in which the priest has literally to let himself be carried by the *instituteur*). In *Manon des sources*, the *instituteur* pits rational materialist instruction against the superstitions of the villagers, those of the Church included. In *César*, it is M. Brun and the Doctor who fill the position of the *instituteur*: the former offers instruction (explaining the chemical properties of alcohol, correcting linguistic error); the latter argues directly with the priest, deploring the alarm caused by his presence at the bedside of the sick (there is an echo here of the confrontation between the pharmacist and the priest in Flaubert's *Madame Bovary* as they watch over Emma's

The doctor takes the priest firmly to task

corpse; save that, for Flaubert, the pharmacist's materialist certitudes are as platitudinous as the priest's spiritual ones).

Family Matters

The trilogy turns on a father who with all the force of his brutal love dominates an adult son whom he thereby deprives of any independence and on a young, unmarried woman expecting a baby. The relation between father and son – or father and daughter – and the predicament of the single mother are recurrent in Pagnol's work, with the two sometimes conflated as the drama of a father's violent reaction to his single-mother daughter (in *Angèle*, the daughter is forced to live hidden in a cellar with her baby). These themes are there in the trilogy in the context of an *absence* of family: César has no wife, Honorine no husband; while Marius and Fanny have no siblings and face their father or mother on their own. The family void is filled by César as a kind of tribal chief, interfering in everything and demanding everyone's obedience.

There is a comic side to this and the interactions between father and son, mother and daughter, César and the Vieux-Port extended family are the occasion for much traditional humour, often concerned with cuckolds and mistresses and producing a kind of absence-of-family burlesque. A famous scene in *Marius* has César attempting casually to set off for his supposedly secret weekly rendezvous with his mistress only to be stopped in his self-conscious tracks by a barrage of knowingly innocent questions from M. Brun. The scene is rhymingly repeated later in the film when Marius, affecting nonchalance, sets off to be with Fanny; save that in this instance no one, César least of all, suspects the serious truth, imagines the mistress could be Fanny.

Along with the comedy comes a darker side that the two themes of parent/child and unmarried mother bring with them and that the situation of Fanny and Marius uncovers. The jokes are one thing, but in the background, talked of in the first two films, is the figure of Fanny's Aunt Zoë: young and in love, much like Fanny, she gave herself to a Spanish sailor who returned to sea, leaving her to end as a prostitute, the shame of the family. Family honour is serious and woman's guarantee of that essential. Male jokes about mistresses and cuckolding wives are one thing; the women to whom they refer are comically distant, have no disturbing presence in the films, any more than does the tragic Zoë: they and she are the limits of the films' vision (Richebé in his memoirs published a scene from the script of *Fanny* in which Fanny goes to see Zoë; rightly, this was not included in the film: Zoë is not an individual woman but a cautionary figure). When Fanny pleads to be allowed to stay single, the response is immediate: there is room for only one single-mother – or 'slut' – in a family and Zoë has already taken that place in theirs. César, learning from Honorine that she has found Fanny and Marius in bed, tells his son Zoë's sad story and sternly, scornfully, enjoins him to marry Fanny without delay: 'if you want my view ... Zoë's sailor was no man'.

Sex as such is not a problem. No one thinks it morally wrong that Fanny and Marius have 'anticipated' marriage. When Honorine flies into a rage after discovering them together, César reminds her that *she* had anticipated her marriage, provoking a reply comically concerned solely with hair-splitting notions of respectability: 'It wasn't the same thing ... we lived on the same landing and there was only a corridor to cross ... and it was me who went to him.' The rage concerns family honour; the more so here in the context of the reality of the Vieux-Port. Elzéar's is a parish of 'unfortunate women' and the fall from innocence to shame would have been visible in the streets surrounding the bar and is glimpsed very occasionally in the film in exterior shots of women standing in doorways or being accosted by sailors. Hence the importance of the dividing line of reputation. For Honorine, there is one stark alternative: either Fanny marries or she ends up like Zoë, her reputation gone and nothing left to lose – as César tells Marius, 'honour is like matches, it can only be used once'.

Women

It was Renoir's opinion that Pagnol considered women 'only useful for having children' and friends commented on his difficulty in conceiving of equality for the sexes (the breakdown of his relationship with Orane Demazis seems to have owed much to this). Films and plays are not short of misogynistic comments: 'You are intelligent to the extent to which a woman can be intelligent,' Demazis's script-girl character is told in *Le Schpountz* and Pagnol's own view of women can at times seem not much different, with the central women characters brought to their proper fulfilment in love and marriage. At the same time, their treatment overall is often uncertain, uneasy in a way that the marriage ending cannot always successfully conclude.

Pagnol himself was twice married and had other important relationships; of his five children, three were born out of wedlock and raised by their mothers. No simple parallel can be drawn between his films and his life: there is a social divide between the author's biographical reality and the Vieux-Port world of the shellfish-stall girl or the Provençal village of the peasant's daughter in *Angèle* or the well-digger's in *La Fille du puisatier*. Yet this theme, this particular figure of the *fille-mère*, clearly comes close to him. In *César*, as in *La Fille du puisatier*, the woman finally marries the father of her child; in *Angèle*, she marries the man who truly loved her and who tried to warn her against the Marseille crook by whom she is seduced into prostitution and whose child she bears. All three endure a period of punishment for their 'fault': Angèle and Patricia, the well-digger's daughter, are repudiated for a time by their fathers; Fanny has to give up on her love and marry Panisse.

Three of Pagnol's relationships were with women who were leading actresses in his films: Orane Demazis, the mother of his first child, Josette Day and Jacqueline Bouvier, the mother of his last two children. All were cinematically rewarded by Pagnol. Demazis's success in cinema was largely in roles written for her by Pagnol. Day, a child actor in a couple of silent films, had started a career as a dancer before returning to cinema in the early 1930s; unlike Demazis, she had known considerable film success prior to her title role in *La Fille du puisatier* and her subsequent establishment as the object of Pagnol's infatuation and glorification in issue after issue of the second series of *Les Cahiers du film*. Bouvier had appeared in a few minor films but success came in films written for her by Pagnol, again in cinematic adoration (his adaptation of Schubert's song-cycle *Die Schöne Müllerin* being the most desperate; *La Belle meunière*, 1948).

A shift can be seen in the nature of the roles given these women. Demazis's key roles (Fanny, Angèle, Arsule in *Regain*, 1937) are women who suffer as a result of men and are more or less submissive to them (though Fanny develops in independence). Jacqueline Pagnol (as Bouvier becomes after *Naïs*, 1945) is, supremely, Manon in *Manon des sources*: the beautiful, free-spirited woman who, scorning the narrow-minded peasant world around her, lives wild in the hills until tamed by the Pagnol *instituteur* figure and settled with him. Significantly, between Demazis and Bouvier-Pagnol, Day in 1941 is subject and object of the awkward hymn to love that *La Prière aux étoiles* would have been. Her role was that of a woman who has made her way through a series of liaisons and whose ambition is to be a film star; an ambition to which her current lover panders by secretly financing films in which she can appear,

Orane Demazis (right) in
Angèle

Josette Day (front right) in *La
Fille du puisatier* (with Raimu
centre and Fernandel to his
right)

Jacqueline Pagnol in Pagnol's
second *Topaze*, 1950 (with
Fernandel)

eventually setting up a production company to make them. She, deep down, prays for the true love we are destined by the stars (hence the film's title). When her prayer is granted, she drops everything to be with the embodiment of this stellar love but he, discovering her past of lovers *and cinema*, repudiates her. Learning she is expecting his child and living far from Paris, he takes her back and they embrace their destiny away from it all and, more especially, from cinema. It would be hard to deny that this extended film fantasy is bound up with the Pagnol–Day relationship and that its elements – a man offering films to the woman he adores, anxieties concerning her past lovers and her use of them, doubts around cinema, retreat to a small town near Marseille (Cassis, which figures in some versions of *César*) – are not expressive of a certain disturbance.

Pagnol celebrates 'his' women, puts them into his cinema, while at the same time holding to an idea of love and woman that stands opposed to cinema (in which that idea is nevertheless expressed). Day is cinematically adored only for the film of that adoration to suggest distrust of women and cinema and to give us a Pagnol split in two: the lover who gives her cinema, this film, along with the anti-cinema lover who holds on to an idealisation of love and to the woman–mother as the fact of the ideal, pure of the world. It is not really surprising that Pagnol planned a film to be called *Le Premier amour* that was to have depicted the 'pre-historical' awakening of love.

Lying

A large part is played in the trilogy and above all in *César* by *lying*, both as a factor in the drama and as a source of comedy. In *César* alone, we have *inter alia*: César asking Elzéar not to frighten Panisse by arriving in full priestly robes for the last rites but to pretend to have happened to be passing ('It's a lie I'm asking of you'); Elzéar doing so ('You're a liar and it's obvious,' Panisse retorts); Panisse confessing to 'the sin of lying' ('Business wouldn't be possible if one always had to tell the truth to one's clients'); and the Doctor insisting on the need to lie to the sick. These examples are of a kind of accepted, everyday lying, usually proposed as humanly better than telling the truth: the sick ought to be reassured, not upset with the facts of their condition. Even Panisse's view of the commercial necessity of lying remains unquestioned in the context of the comedy in which it is set (César nods agreement, the priest makes no confessional objection). Naturally, this conventional, *sociable* lying is recognised as such: the lies merely express the truth they seek to hide.

Panisse is nowise duped by priest or doctor: their lies tell him he is near death every bit as much as does Césariot's truthful declaration that he has come from Paris because of his father's critical condition. All of which amounts to a humorous representation of the argument between Immanuel Kant and Benjamin Constant: the absolute duty to speak the truth versus a pragmatic calculation of effects, the recognition that lying may in certain circumstances be the course of action best allowing fulfilment of one's duty to others.

The Chauffeur performs lying

Lying also features as something of a way of life, practised by the characters and enjoyed by the audience. This is made explicit in *César* in the scene in which Fanny questions the Chauffeur about the destination of Césariot's planned boat trip. In answer, he *performs* lying, going into a comic turn of exaggerated gestures, oaths on his parents' grave, and vehement protestations that he would go through the war again rather than lie – 'Especially since you weren't in the war', Fanny tartly replies. Asked why he lies, the Chauffeur replies simply 'for pleasure' and many of the trilogy's scenes depend for their comedy on just such a pleasure. 'Naturally I take you for a liar,' Panisse reassures Escartefigue after the latter has told a particularly outrageous story in *Fanny*; and when, in *Marius*, M. Brun reports on Paris as being 'more than twice [the size of] Marseille', he too is naturally taken as a liar and granted comic approval. In *César* the Chauffeur, maintaining the lie that Césariot is visiting Dromart, phones and pretends to be watching the two of them playing bowls; at the other end, César and Dromart himself (!) listen in amusement, showing no sign of outrage; just as the Chauffeur enjoys his performance, so do they and we too, taken by the sheer comic effrontery of it all as the film cuts in turn from one end of the phone to the other.

There are also, however, serious, structuring lies, deviations from the truth that impel the drama. Fanny lies to Marius about her intentions regarding Panisse; Marius is kept uninformed of the birth of his son (an example of what Elzéar calls 'lying by dissimulation'); Césariot is kept ignorant of the fact that he is Marius's son ('You lied to me for twenty years,' he reproaches Fanny). The drama of *César* stems from the revelation of the truth to Césariot which, ironically, leads to more lies along the way to the film's resolution. Césariot lies to Fanny when he goes to Toulon to check on Marius and lies to the latter by withholding his true

The Chauffeur's stories …   … amuse César and Dromart

identity, thus laying himself open to Fernand's lies about Marius's supposed criminal activities. In *César* indeed, only Marius and Fanny are not actively involved in lying – Césariot's bitter 'What am I going to think of women now that I know my mother can lie!' is wrong: Fanny told Panisse of her pregnancy before their marriage.

Without the lies and dissimulations there would be no revelation, no drama, no films. Pagnol's problem in *César* was how to conduct the revelation, how to give it form and establish the sense it makes of this film and the behaviour of the trilogy's characters. That this was a problem is indicated by the different versions of it there are, as though Pagnol were unsure as to quite where to locate the demand that the truth be told. In the film as we have it, neither Fanny nor, even less, Panisse express any desire to tell Césariot of his true paternity. They are enjoined to do so by the priest, Elzéar, in order of all things to avoid incest (Marius might have a daughter whom Césariot might meet and half-brother and half-sister might marry unknowingly). Panisse is distraught at the prospect of losing 'his' son through such truth-telling and utters an anguished 'non, non, non' before pathetically burying himself under the sheets. It is Fanny who, the evening after the funeral, tells Césariot, stressing she is doing so only at Elzéar's command: 'he has forced me to say that you are not Honoré's son'. In the first film version, Elzéar similarly invokes incest as justification for the revelation in a longer scene of heated argument between him and Panisse. The revelation is made two weeks later: Fanny and Césariot are at the family villa in Cassis and Elzéar comes to urge her to tell him. The same scenario is found in the 1937 printed 'text of the film', save that there, given Panisse's refusal, Elzéar announces he will return the next day so that they can reach agreement and complete the confession – but Panisse dies in the meantime in the 'state of mortal sin' that Elzéar threatened would be his fate were the confession not completed; when Elzéar later turns up in Cassis, he assures Fanny that she will 'leave Honoré in purgatory' if she fails to tell Césariot. The 1947 text of the play simply eliminates the whole confession; Fanny tells Césariot just after the funeral in fulfilment of a promise to Panisse who 'forced me to reveal that you are not his son'; Elzéar appears only briefly at the beginning of the scene to overcome her reluctance to keep the promise – 'What use will it have?'. More changes occur in the revised, 'film made in 1936' text. In this, Panisse tells Elzéar that he wishes to correct 'a daily lie that has gone on for twenty years' and entrusts him with a letter – a few lines 'to prove that his mother never lied to me' – that is eventually to be given to Fanny to give to Césariot. Elzéar, here shown more sympathetically, uttering no threats of incest or damnation, delivers the letter to Fanny in Cassis two years later and asks that she honour Panisse's wish. This she does, again questioning the point of it – 'Why tell him since he's happy?' – and reflecting on 'our lie' – 'It was not a crime. It was in the child's interest ...'

In none of the versions is it Fanny who wants the revelation to be made, though, subject to priest's or husband's male authority, it is always she who has to declare the lie, laying herself open thereby to her son's questioning of her truth as wife, mother, woman. Fanny, indeed, is the crux of a *friction* of values. She has committed a 'fault', or what became such when Marius's departure put paid to their envisaged marriage, and this must be made good by the marriage to Panisse which banishes the spectre of Aunt Zoë. Césariot is the evidence of both the fault and its reparation, the latter depending on the redemptive lie (that Panisse is his father).

Fanny's question as to the point now of telling the truth is much of the drama of *César*: the film picks up the lying that has run through the trilogy and makes the process of its correction the means of resolution: the truth leads Césariot to the truth of Marius (after the unscrambling of Fernand's diversionary lies) and Marius back to Fanny and the truth of their love. At the same time, however, Elzéar's rather surprising warnings in some versions about the danger of incest confusedly pull the fault deeper. His incest obsession, after all, hits its mark not as regards Césariot and his hypothetical half-sister but as regards Césariot as himself a product of incest. Much emphasis is put on Fanny and Marius's common childhood, their brother-and-sister closeness: asked by Panisse whether Marius is in love with Fanny, César replies 'Oh no, they've known each other too long!', and Marius declares that he considers Fanny as his sister; to which she replies, 'I don't want to be your sister ... ', but then she *is*, is half a sister at least.

Fanny's question is a good one: why give up the pragmatic lie? Césariot is happy believing Panisse to be his father (and in human terms, after all, Panisse *is* his father); moreover, he seems no happier as a result of having been told the truth which effectively excludes him, leaving him there at the close only in César's report of his chilling acceptance of Fanny and

Marius marrying: 'There are three solutions: either mother grows old alone, and if I marry one day, she'll poison my wife's life; or she'll gallivant around with him, having secret meetings in sad hotel rooms; or they'll get married. I prefer they get married.'

That he disappears is as it should be: the trilogy's drama concerns Fanny and Marius and the point of the revelation is the truth of Fanny, not Césariot. We could think of the problem the films raise as that of *being-Fanny*: what is it to be Fanny? In *Marius*, it is to be a girl-woman who occupies her expected position and manifests any independence within the conventions of the feminine. From earliest childhood, as César stresses in *Marius*, she loves a young man who loves her but who now looks outwards, beyond her. As they sit side by side, Fanny plans the furnishing of their future bedroom while Marius stares off-screen, alert only to the sirens of departing ships. She wants no more than marriage and the continuation of their Vieux-Port life; indeed, once married, they are to live with César in the bar. Finally, she sacrifices herself for him and then does so again for her son by marrying Panisse. In *Fanny*, until she gives birth (a pivotal moment), she plays much the same role, thereafter asserting herself as a well-off, married, business woman. In *César*, after Panisse's death, her old feelings come to the surface again, demanding an ending that reunites her with Marius.

Fanny's material independence as Panisse's widow is accompanied by a strong affirmation of her as a woman with sexual desires and rights. This is touched on comically in one of the trilogy's rare instances of risqué humour. The Chauffeur, waiting in the boat to set off with Césariot, greets Fanny as 'belle plante', common as an expression for a good-looking woman; she bridles at this, whereupon he launches into praise of the cleanness – the *propreté* – of the boat, also called '*Fanny*', with a double entendre account of its readiness: 'Our *Fanny* has never been so beautiful. All she needs is a good turn of the starting handle on the sensitive spot and, hop, off we go! Full steam ahead!' (The name 'Fanny' itself has its own local double entendre: *baiser Fanny* – to fuck Fanny – was an expression in bowls meaning to lose the game without scoring any points. Supposedly, the expression's origin involved a bar and the beautiful woman named Fanny who ran it: if one had a bad game, consolation might be possible with Fanny. Inevitably enough, at the time of the trilogy there was a registered Marseille bowls club called La Fanny.) That Fanny is 'clean' is a given; it is the word Panisse urges on

Césariot: 'One day he said to me: "She is intelligent ... she is devoted ... she is clean ... Clean, that's the word", he said.'

It is indeed, and echoes through the revelation scene as Césariot imagines the worst of his mother's behaviour, provoking her into an impassioned affirmation of her desires. Marriage to Panisse kept her 'clean', spared her Aunt Zoë's fate, but, at the cost of giving up on her sexuality, a sexuality that, in the face of Césariot's cruel misgivings, she refuses to accept as negative. The prohibition on unclean sexuality – the projection of incest on to Marius and Fanny through their children – disappears. Twenty years have paid for their fault and they can start again; Césariot drops out and, César insists, there will be new children: it is all cleaned up. But not quite: after all, being Fanny is what exactly? The happy submission to César as he remakes the couple she wanted so long ago? The force of the sexual desire she claims ('the taste of sin' she radiantly recalls experiencing with Marius)? The extraordinarily vehement sexual disgust she startlingly expresses when she suspects Césariot of having been with a woman ('You'll do me the pleasure of seeing the doctor and he's to examine you all over. And you're going to give me what you're wearing so I can disinfect it ... Go and undress')?

Tragedy, Comedy

'It is scene of tragedy ... yes, tragedy', declares the Chauffeur in the play *Fanny*, as he and the others contemplate the spectacle of César devastated by Marius's departure. Tragedy, however, turns quickly to the comedy of their nervous attempts to get him to 'clear his mind' (or 'open the valve', as Escartefigue professionally puts it). For Pagnol, the difference between tragedy and comedy was 'very simple'. There is, he wrote in the preface to the play *César*, just one dramatic subject: man loves woman; an obstacle comes between them; marriage or death are the only outcomes ('pointless looking for others, the public doesn't like them'): 'If they marry, it's a comedy; if not, it's a tragedy'. In conversation he was cruder: 'When the curtain goes up, the question is posed: will they fuck? If they do, it's a comedy; if not it's a drama'.

For Fanny and Marius the outcome is marriage, not death, but *César* knows no sharp division between tragedy and comedy and cannot be neatly fitted to Pagnol's formula. The question about them fucking was answered in *Marius* and hardly put paid to tragic effects; on the contrary, the sexual union led to the subsequent drama and the trilogy's films are edged with shadows; increasingly so as we move from Marius's painful departure to Fanny's suffering, the drama of his return, their second parting, the death of Panisse, and the bitter rehearsal of the rights and wrongs of past events.

'Ça, c'est trop beau,' comments a character in *Angèle* on hearing of something that bodes well for a happy ending. As in a way it is too much, is *trop beau*. The comment is immediately and, in the Pagnol world, inevitably translated into a popular figurative language which comically draws attention to the 'too muchness': 'Il y a de quoi se taper le cul dans un seau,' quite enough indeed to make one stick one's arse in a bucket for joy. 'Nous voilà en plein pastis sentimental,' César sighs when Césariot turns up late at night having learnt that he is Marius's son, and yes we are, are in a right pathetic, comic, painful mess; as we often are in the trilogy with its particular melodramatic mix of laughter and tears. Pagnol had a strong admiration for Dickens and if the trilogy lacks anything of the latter's exploration of the dark depths of city life, it does share the mingling of comic and tragic, character humour and emotional drama; as it shares too Dickens's wishful creation of little worlds apart, pockets of feeling which evade too much reality – the bar and its inhabitants go on with a cheerful familiarity that keeps us on course for the happy ending in which, finally, the whole sentimental melodrama will seemingly come to rest.

Pagnol, in fact, is never far from the speech on laughter that the script-girl (Orane Demazis) in *Le Schpountz* delivers to the cinema-obsessed simpleton (Fernandel, the 'schpountz' of the title), whom a film crew pretend to take seriously in his belief that he has the makings of a great dramatic actor. The scene they film with him is greeted as uproariously funny, plunging him into a state of despondency that the script-girl seeks to alleviate with a celebration of comedy: 'Don't speak ill of laughter. It doesn't exist in nature: trees don't laugh and animals don't know how to laugh ... Only humans laugh ... Laughter is a human thing, a virtue belonging only to humans and given them perhaps by God to console them for being intelligent.'

The trilogy enshrines this virtue, with laughter always close to the drama and allowed free rein in many scenes. The most famous of these is that in *Marius* in which César, Panisse, Escartefigue and M. Brun are playing cards in the bar. Escartefigue, partnered with César, is hesitant as to what he should play and César, exasperated, tries by a series of egregious hints to convey to him that Panisse trumps with hearts; giving César one of the trilogy's most famous lines: 'il me fend le COEUR', he's breaking my HEART; apparently an expression of the hurt he feels that Panisse is watching him for foul play but really a hint to Escartefigue. Panisse takes offence at this cheating and leaves, prompting César to another famous line: 'If you can't cheat with your friends, there's no point in playing cards any more.' The game continues until César, speculating that Marius's supposed mistress must be a sailor's wife, declares that 'everyone knows it's in the navy you find the most cuckolds'; at which Escartefigue too goes off in a huff, offended not because he is a cuckold but because, as a sea-faring man (captain of the Vieux-Port ferry!), he resents the insult to the navy. César's propitiatory protestations of admiration for the latter merely provoke Escartefigue to yet another famous line: 'Perhaps you do like the French navy but to you the French navy says *merde*.'

The scene is done again in *César* in one of the rhyming repetitions that bind the trilogy. The funeral over, César, Escartefigue and M. Brun are again playing cards in the bar, having dealt a hand for Panisse as though he were still with them. As the game proceeds, they make conjectures as to how he would have played, falling silent as the reality of his empty chair comes home to them but soon picking up the game again, excitedly playing out his winning hand. Cinematically, the scene is more adventurous than its counterpart in *Marius*. It opens with an extreme high-angle shot on to the table at which the three are sitting (the Doctor is present too, a little to the rear), powerfully establishing the emptiness of Panisse's chair, and continues with shot/counter-shot sequences moving between characters' points of view and the point of view from the empty chair, at once putting us in the dead man's place and holding us to the sight of his absence. The comic card game in *Marius* is turned into one of visual emotion as we cross from the comedy of the game to the chair's materialisation of death

The card game and the pathos of the empty chair

Lumière's *Partie d'écarté*

(César: 'I hadn't yet realised he was dead'); but with comedy returning to heighten the emotion as Panisse is made vividly present through the excited playing of his hand. With consummate pathos, Pagnol closes the game on Panisse's voice, as though he were present speaking: realistically, it is César imitating Panisse, yet no shot fixes the voice as César's; we hear it on the soundtrack over an emphatic shot of the empty chair and, watching in the cinema, it is not so easy to distinguish it from Panisse's own; which difficulty is the point, is the emotion.

Pagnol had initially decided to omit the card-game scene from *Marius*, only to have it reinstated by Raimu. His doubts were motivated by its similarity to scenes in the highly popular vaudeville theatre of Georges Courteline. Indeed *Boubouroche* (1893), Courteline's first big success, opens precisely with four friends playing cards in a café and contains several elements that appear in Pagnol's scene. It is not that Pagnol explicitly copied Courteline but that the vaudeville theatre was important in his work (one of his first films, *L'Article 330*, 1934, was an adaptation of a Courteline farce) and this seems to have given rise at the start of his career to schpountz-like misgivings; he was, after all, ambitious for recognition as a *serious* dramatist. The scene's cinematic reference is to the first film card game, Louis Lumière's *Partie d'écarté*, shot in La Ciotat in 1895, which has three men round a table, two of them playing a game of écarté, and a waiter who brings drinks and laughs; laughs in anticipation, as I like to think, of Pagnol's two great comic – but in *César* much more than comic – card-game scenes.

4

. . . .

MARSEILLE

Godard's *À Bout de souffle* (1959) opens with a gangster and his girlfriend stealing a car from a couple of American tourists on the Quai des Belges before heading for Paris. Fittingly enough, one of the defining films of the cinematically self-conscious *nouvelle vague* thus begins on the Vieux-Port, the central location of Marseille's presence in cinema and of its cinematic myth. The opening is fitting too in its recognition of the city's importance in the history of cinema: as setting and source of subjects and genres, and, at times, as a centre of film-making activity (as Pagnol's own film company testifies).

In the first decades of the twentieth century, Marseille was France's second city, its first maritime port, and its great 'colonial metropolis': 'the door of the fatherland opening onto its empire overseas', as the city's chamber of commerce proudly proclaimed. It was also a major industrial centre – 'always covered in smoke', Pagnol remembered – with oil distilleries, sugar refineries, flour mills, soap factories, and so on. There was a measure of economic growth after World War I and for a while, the effects of the Depression were felt less than elsewhere in France, with the city wearing an appearance of prosperity triumphantly displayed in its two Colonial Exhibitions of 1906 and 1922. The city had drawn heavily on immigrant labour for its development and this continued to be the case in the years of Pagnol's youth and those of the trilogy. The abundance of

À Bout de souffle: Belmondo ready to leave the Vieux-Port

such cheap labour, however, kept the city's industries going without providing incentive for modernisation and, as a result of this and the increasing effects of the Depression, the 1930s saw a slowing down of production. The city itself, moreover, had failed to deal with the problems resulting from its growth and relative prosperity had been accompanied by a conflicting reality of social poverty and urban degradation (naturally, immigrants were often regarded as a major cause of this degradation). The largest concentrations of workers were found in districts north of the Vieux-Port – 'where the true proletariat begins', Walter Benjamin reported after a visit in 1928.

The city's population in 1931, the year of *Marius*, was around 800,000, with immigrants representing close to twenty per cent of that number; Italians were by far the largest group, with Armenians, Spaniards and North Africans making up other significant but smaller groups. The numbers in transit at any given time need also to be remembered: new immigrants arriving or passing through, sailors on shore leave, travellers of every kind, all intermingling in what Benjamin called 'the belly of the city': the relatively small space of the Vieux-Port where, it was commonly said, could be seen all the faces and peoples of the earth, though not in the trilogy, where all those with any individualised role are white and where only a very tiny number of non-European faces are glimpsed among the people seen in shots of the streets near César's bar.

Le Vieux-Port

Siegfried Kracauer writing for the *Frankfurter Zeitung* in 1926 described the sea as pushing into the city, forming a kind of liquid town square with quays and their buildings on three of its sides: on one side, the Quai du Port; on the opposite side, the Quai de Rive Neuve; at one end, facing out to the open sea at the other, the Quai des Belges, into and from which runs the Canebière, the city's great central avenue, what Kracauer called 'the street of streets'. César has his bar on the Quai de Rive Neuve, as Panisse has his sail-making establishment, and as Honorine and Fanny have their fish stalls. The mid-nineteenth century had seen the start of the construction of new docks able to accommodate the great steamships now dominant in merchant shipping and, by the time of the trilogy, the Vieux-Port had lost much of its economic importance (Kracauer thought it 'abandoned'). What activity remained centred around fishing-boats,

The *Malaisie* sets sail with
Marius aboard

Marius's bedroom: the pictures
of sail …

… and steam

sailing-ships, steamships of modest tonnage, and ferries (today, more marina than port, it is given over to yachts and tourist-trip boats). The *Malaisie*, the great three-master on which Marius leaves to fulfil his dream of the sea, existed and had put in to Marseille in the years of Pagnol's youth (though contrary to what is suggested in one of the opening shots of *Fanny*, it seems not to have been a Marseille ship); by the time of the trilogy, however, such ships were largely a thing of the past. Pointedly, in *Marius* the camera lingers on two pictures in Marius's bedroom: one of just such a sailing ship, the other of a steamship; the dream is with the former, the reality with the latter. We might also note here, as regards the dream, that Marius is a somewhat untypical Marseillais: the Marseille-born writer Alfred Suarès, along with many others, was adamant that 'most of the children here have no dream of seeing the world'; an attitude reflected in César's stupefaction in *Marius* at the idea that anyone could want to go to sea ('impossible to play a game of bowls!') and Escartefigue's declaration that, though proud to be a sailor, he has no intention of navigating beyond the Vieux-Port ('Go out to sea? ON A BOAT? No thanks!').

Pagnol himself hated sea travel and travel generally (the trip to London for *The Broadway Melody* was exceptional). His sights as a young man had been set inland, on leaving Marseille *for Paris*. Writing *Marius*, however, prompted a certain imaginative return. In a later preface to the play, he noted that he had thought to have little liking for the city: 'The Vieux-Port seemed to me dirty – and it was; as for what was picturesque about the old districts, it had hardly affected me until then, and the charm of the little streets cluttered with rubbish had always escaped me. But absence often reveals to us what we love ...' What absence revealed to him was 'the joyful populace of fishermen and fishwomen', 'the smell of those shops ... where in the shadows can be seen coils of rope, folded sails on shelves and big copper lanterns hung from the ceiling', 'the little shady bars along the quayside' and 'the fresh Marseille women at the fish stalls'; which is to say that it revealed the world conjured up in the trilogy: Panisse's shop, César's bar, Honorine's and Fanny's stalls.

Yet it was the dirtiness that contemporaries regularly stressed. Benjamin recorded 'a stink of oil, urine, and printer's ink' from 'newspaper kiosks, lavatories, and oyster stalls', the latter, unlike Fanny's, with 'warty mountains of pink shellfish' on 'dirty planks' awash with an 'unfathomable wetness'. The port was 'a gullet' opening to catch 'the black and brown proletarian bodies thrown to it' and the harbour people were 'a bacillus culture, the porters and whores products of decomposition'. The degradation, that is, was moral too. For Suarès, writing in 1931, the Vieux-Port was 'the meeting-place of pleasure and dissipation', and Benjamin paused on the 'discoloured women' found 'strategically placed' in 'this depot of worn-out alleyways'. On the Quai du Port side was the Quartier Réservé, made up of such alleyways, where by municipal decree brothels were tolerated and where the number of prostitutes at the time of the trilogy is estimated to have been considerably over a thousand (certain brothels showed pornographic films, many of them according to Pagnol produced in Marseille). Along with prostitution, went an underworld of crime, to which the shifting population of immigrants and sailors could be quickly linked in fact and fiction.

A report in early 1943 noted that the Vieux-Port's reputation as 'the most dangerous criminal centre in the world' was reductive and described it as inhabited 'in large part by fishermen, artisans and peaceful elements'. The report is eminently believable (and archival research anyway confirms its truth) since it was written by the German consul in Marseille to his Paris superiors at the very time when those superiors were planning to cleanse the city of what they regarded as its running sore of impurity and criminality by destroying a section of the Vieux-Port: the whole of the Quartier Réservé. The destruction was carried out early in 1943 when French police, backed by German soldiers, rounded up Jews living there for deportation, evacuated everyone else and dynamited some 1,500 buildings, leaving only the Hôtel de Ville and one or two façades fronting onto the Quai du Maréchal Pétain, as the Quai du Port had been renamed.

The trilogy *is* Marseille in Pagnol's film work. *Merlusse* was filmed in the Lycée Thiers of his adolescent years but its sentimental Christmas story depends little on particular location in Marseille. When the city does occasionally enter other films, it is in terms of dirtiness and corruption. In *Angèle*, Marseille is where the village girl is forced into prostitution and from where she is rescued by a simple-minded, true-hearted farmhand (Fernandel) whom we see finding his way through the unknown streets to the hotel-brothel which has become her home. Otherwise, Marseille is outside Pagnol's cinema, there only in scattered remarks made by characters, almost invariably hostile. Even before completing the trilogy – witness *Angèle* – Pagnol had begun the turn inland to the *arrière-pays*, leaving Marseille as negative representation, anti-value. Nowhere is this more forcefully expressed than in the farmhand's speech to Angèle when he finally registers what she has become: 'Listen, miss, one evening I was walking by the Marseille canal: I dipped my hand in the water. It was a heavy, lukewarm, sluggish water … Whereas at home, up on the mountain, … the water is pure … quick and cold, a water that pushes your hand … Come with me, miss.' The trilogy's village – for what it presents is a kind of village community within the Vieux-Port – has gone elsewhere, Pagnol's setting now the villages and hills of the Provence that he will provide with what Bazin was to characterise as 'its universal epic', *Manon des sources*.

César marks this shift. If the trilogy begins with Marius and Fanny on the Vieux-Port, it comes to an end in the country, beyond the Vieux-Port to which it seems unable to return us, though we are supposed to believe that Fanny and Marius will continue their life there. It is as if the Vieux-Port of the three films has been the lengthy pause of an anachronistic world now being brought to a conclusion at the moment of Pagnol's relocation of his films to a sensually austere Provence untroubled by the confusions of the city that the trilogy holds at bay. In *Cigalon*, a crooked Marseille bookmaker, speaking of gangsters from whom he is hiding, says: 'It seems that the day they prepared the robbery, it was in a bar in the port'; such a bar, such an idea of the port, as the trilogy refuses (difficult to imagine anything more than a game of bowls being plotted in César's bar!) – *that* Marseille was another cinema.

The final shot: Marius and Fanny go off into the country

Marseille and cinema go together from the start; early Lumière *vues* of the Vieux-Port and the Canebière quickly put the city into film and the development of film production locally in the 1910s and 20s saw an increasing number of films shot and indeed set in Marseille; certain of which were and remain significant works: Louis Delluc's *Fièvre* (1921), Jean Epstein's *Cœur fidèle* (1923), Alberto Cavalcanti's *En Rade* (1927); melodramas that draw on and create the atmosphere of the port. *En Rade* turns on the same desire for elsewhere that will inflame Marius; *Fièvre* and *Cœur fidèle* are set in a Vieux-Port quayside bar and involve men linked with the sea and jealous clashes over women. Delluc's film was originally to be called *La Boue* (literally 'mud'), an indication of the mode of realism of these films, of the darkness of their worlds of the lower depths.

(top) *Fièvre*: Vieux-Port fights and prostitutes; (above) *Le Club des fadas*: Vieux-Port fun and games   63

Aspects of the trilogy can be found in these silent films: *Fièvre*, for example, opens with a group in the bar playing cards and a woman whose lover has left her for the sea. Pagnol's trilogy films, of course, are a very different cinema, at once in style – the films of Delluc (especially), Epstein and Cavalcanti are classics of an avant-garde French cinema of the silent era – and in vision – the darkness has gone (though present in the negative comments on Marseille in other Pagnol films) and the Vieux-Port is light with comedy and sentiment. The trilogy's roots are in a local music-hall tradition that exploits the verve and accent and humour of Marseille popular speech and that the coming of sound cinematically enables. The trilogy brings this tradition into film, providing it with its influential cinematic and cultural definition, Indeed, it largely creates a vogue for Marseille and Marseillais 'characters' manifested above all in the development of a Marseille comic genre, for which Marseille is not so much a city but a theatre of sketches and songs played out in increasingly familiar settings. This is the genre exemplified in films like *Le Club des fadas* (Emile Couzinet, 1938) and *Un de la Canebière* (René Pujol, 1938): the former involving a group of Marseillais bent on fun; the latter a quid pro quo comedy with music-hall songs. The trilogy permeates such films: in *Un de la Canebière* the ferry-boat captain has become a tramway driver played by the same actor (Paul Dullac) in much the same role – and with similar scenes and cuckoldry jokes.

Marseille Myth

Pagnol reinforces and defines a certain mythology of Marseille and its people developed between the wars. This had earlier beginnings, bound up more generally with a conception of the Midi given decisive national expression in Alphonse Daudet's *Lettres de mon moulin* (1869) and *Tartarin de Tarascon* (1872). Daudet fixed the idea of the region's people as 'lively, animated, loquacious, exaggerative, comic, impressionable'; adjectives which fit the trilogy's characters and are essential to the form of the myth in which Daudet and Pagnol after him had a strong creative hand (Pagnol wrote scenario and dialogue for a 1934 film of *Tartarin de Tarascon* starring Raimu and directed *Lettres de mon moulin* for the screen in 1954). To think of a Marseillais in the 1930s and thereafter is typically to think of a hyperbolic pantomime of gestures, expressions and emotions in Daudet's and the trilogy's terms. As it is to think of such inevitable 'characteristics' as an irrepressible thirst for pastis and an overriding passion for bowls (in *Fanny*, César and co. bring a tram to a halt while they finish a game in the middle of the road), all of them shot through with a particular form of humour: generously ironic, emphatically extravagant, naturally veering to the *galéjade* – the tall story, the practical joke (for 'fishing and the *galéjade*, we're the best', a character proudly declares in *Un de la Canebière*).

Pagnol, for whom there was 'no art outside of commonplaces', catches up and moulds stereotypes into a popular representation that comes to stand as an accepted reality of Marseille and the Marseillais. Through the power of its story and its actor-characters, the trilogy set the terms of a constant imagination – a 'truth' – of Marseille and the Marseillais, crystallising a folklore that *stuck*. 'Marseille forgets Pagnol' ran a recent headline in *Le Monde* over a piece about the city's bid to host the America's Cup, meaning of course that Pagnol is not at all forgotten, that the effect of the trilogy is still powerful for the imagination of the city. Pagnol's Vieux-Port continues as cultural commonplace and as source for a nostalgic simplicity which is ingenuously rendered in *Les Rois du sport* (Pierre Colombier, 1937), another of those Marseille comic genre films that followed in the wake of the trilogy's success. Two barmen – Raimu and Fernandel – go off to Paris but return in the end to Marseille, for, as Raimu says: 'Here's our bar, the bar we should never have left.' As Marius should never have left: the bar and the Vieux-Port remain the emotional centre to which he too finally returns from his 'exile'.

It is in the 1920s and 30s that the image of Marseille and its inhabitants was powerfully constructed in and through cinema, with the trilogy playing the decisive role in the establishment of its comic, affectionate form. At the same time, the opposite vision of Marseille was also being consolidated, that in which the Vieux-Port is a very different commonplace: the common *place* of a night-time underworld of gangsters, prostitutes, immigrants and marginals moving through narrow, rubbish-strewn streets into brothels and bars (bars, it should be said, are an obligatory location for all Marseille films, whether comic or criminal). The city is narrowed down to this negative representation which then stands for it as inescapably as does its Pagnolesque reverse. The Marseillais Suarès expressed anger that his native city had become 'the most calumnied of all illustrious towns' but, characteristically, himself proceeded to lay on thick descriptions of its horrors, much as did the

Parisian Londres and so many others. Maurice Tourneur's film *Justin de Marseille* (1934) is exemplary in this respect. Its Vieux-Port opening finds a young reporter from Paris in conversation with a local man who complains of the harm done by journalists who propagate stereotypes and see the city only in the light of the expectations created by them. Yet the film itself does just that, itself assuming the stereotype of 'Marseille-Chicago' (a representation opposed by the city authorities who banned the film, quite reasonably unimpressed by the hymn to the beauty of Marseille spoken by the 'good' gangster that the film throws in at the end). Today, new elements have been added and a contemporary imagination constructed around social unrest and racial tension in the northern housing developments: 'Marseille-Chicago' becomes 'Marseille-Beirut' ('Beirut or worse', declares the narrator of Marseille crime novelist Philippe Carrese's *Trois jours d'engatse*; 'it's cinema nonstop').

It is the relation to crime that has been dominant in Marseille's cinema reality since the time of the trilogy (it is this that Godard cites at the start of *À Bout de souffle*). Gangsters, drugs, prostitution, violence are the staple cinema ideas of the city and are found in various combinations in any number of films: *Le Garçon sauvage* (Jean Delannoy,

Justin de Marseille: the
Quartier Réservé ...

... and the pimp and his prey

Marseille crime and
cinema: in *Cap Canaille* the
bullet-torn body lies
sprawled under a plaque
commemorating the
Lumière brothers' invention
of cinema; the plaque was
subsequently removed

1951), *Le Port du désir* (Edmond T. Greville, 1954), *Le Deuxième souffle* (Jean-Pierre Melville, 1966), *Borsalino* (Jacques Deray, 1970), *The French Connection* (William Friedkin, 1971), *Retour à Marseille* (René Allio, 1980), *Cap Canaille* (Juliet Berto, Jean-Henri Roger, 1982), and all the others one could list, through to today and such films as *Total Khéops* (Alain Bévérini, 2002; based on a work by another – the very best – of the contemporary Marseille crime novelists, Jean-Claude Izzo). As for the Marseille music-hall comic genre, that was a phenomenon largely of the 1930s but the appeal of Marseille as a natural setting for and mine of comedy was continued in such films as *Honoré de Marseille* (Maurice Régamey, 1956) and given a new lease of life in the wildly successful *Taxi* (Gérard Pirès, 1998) which slalomed through the Marseille streets, comically finding room on its way for a bit of expected Marseille crime and throwing in some new elements that supplement the old mythology, and first and foremost through its central character: the ferry-boat captain Escartefigue, so to speak, now become a young *beur* – French North-African – taxi-driver.

Marseille Language

With one or two exceptions, the trilogy's characters are *essentially* Marseillais, Marseille is their *country* (in *Le Schpountz*, someone points out that there is no need to worry about the credulous schpountz in Paris since he can easily be 'repatriated' by the 'Marseille consulate' there!). Marseille is not a contingent setting where the films happen to take place but the very foundation of story and characters; indeed, it *is* a character, present throughout in the performed speech of the Marseillais.

Historically, the regional French of Marseille drew on Provençal which was spoken by Pagnol's grandparents and sometimes at home by his father (it had no place in the republican classroom). The Marseillais French familiar to Pagnol was popular French as spoken nationally but informed by regional variations largely stemming from the presence of Provençal. In the language of the trilogy, that presence is there in a number of words by which, within the films' framework of national French popular speech, local particularity is *signified*. This is the effect of interjections – *té* ('tiens'), *vai* ('allez'), *vé* ('regarde'), the all-purpose *peuchère* (from Provençal *pécaïre*; indicating surprise or compassion, but also, contrarily, ironic distance or dismissive scorn) – and of various other words such as *galéjade* and *fada* (soft in the head) scattered through the dialogue. Claudine in *César* produces *embouligue* to specify the cause of her husband's death, confusing Provençal *embouléga* (tangle, muddle) with the French word for embolism and setting off a linguistic comedy as César peremptorily declares the correct term to be the non-existent *embolidre* and as M. Brun is then put down for suggesting, correctly, that the word might be *embolie*: 'Yes, in Lyon' is César's scornful reply. It would be a pity too not to mention *pastis* again: derived from a Provençal word for 'mixture', it was Marseille slang for problem, imbroglio, an inextricable situation, and was then used for the name of the aperitif (because of the troubled, cloudy appearance when water is added), entering national French just as Pagnol was beginning the trilogy. César's 'Nous voilà en plein pastis sentimental' holds both meanings: the situation is a mess and *pastis* is a more than appropriate word in the mouth of a Marseille bar-owner. At particularly difficult moments, one or two of the characters will also drop briefly into dialect: Honorine in *Marius* when overcome by the discovery of Fanny and Marius in bed ('ma pitchouno couchado émè un hommé') or Panisse in *Fanny* when he realises that Fanny may be pregnant ('Es un pitchoun?'). Limited in number, these Provençal words or phrases appear almost solely in the speech of César's generation and are mostly absent from the major dramatic scenes.

It is above all accent that gives the strong Marseille flavour of the trilogy. For Bazin, 'The accent is not in Pagnol a picturesque accessory … a touch of local colour, it is consubstantial with the text and, through that, with the characters … The accent is the very matter of their language, his realism.' True, but Bazin is here talking generally of 'the Pagnol case' (the title of his essay), not specifically of the trilogy in which the accent, like the linguistic particularities, did and does function for audiences as local colour. The idea of its 'realism' also needs qualification. The poet and dramatist Jacques Audiberti once remarked that the people of Marseille learned to speak with their famous accent – 'l'assent' – from going to the cinema to see the trilogy. Which is grossly overstated – Pagnol did not invent the accent! – but has a certain validity nonetheless: the trilogy *established* the accent, made it familiar.

Language and accent are related to social class and dramatic seriousness. The older generation speak with the accent; as does Marius – a *tour de force* on the part of the Parisian Fresnay – but Fanny by the time of *César*, has lost what occasional accent she had (the difference in accent between her and her mother was always strong and we learn that she spent her first twelve years away from Marseille in Algeria, where Demazis herself was born and raised). A major factor here is Fanny's status as heroine and the constraint of a clearly felt convention that the female lead should not be regionally marked. The convention is strikingly observed in *Angèle* and *La Fille du puisatier* where Demazis and Day respectively play heroines without accent despite being the daughters of rough Provençal peasants (the films 'justify' this by informing us that they were brought up away from their families and their region). Whatever accent Fanny had disappears as she becomes effectively middle class and class, of course, is decisive: the Marseille accent gives way to the standard accent as one goes up the social scale, gives way to the speech of the capital, to what the Marseillais César would mockingly call *parler pointu*. Césariot, as befits the recipient of an elite education, speaks 'pointed' Parisian; so much so, César caustically suggests, that to understand him they will soon need an interpreter. Not that the trilogy itself, of course, does not depend on an accepted standard: marked particularities of language and accent must not be allowed overmuch to distract audiences in serious dramatic moments (in 1931 the Marseille music-hall singer Andrée Turcy recorded a song entitled 'J'ai l'accent' recounting the failure of a would-be actress to gain admission to drama academy because of her Marseille accent). There is no attempt at a realism of speech; the local is signified rather than recorded; there are no rough edges, no difficulties of understanding. Yet the trilogy's achievement here should not be underestimated: the accent remains present throughout; as local colour indeed, and as a matter of comedy, but there too in the dramatic scenes. The trilogy, and the more dramatically tensed *César* especially, instate the regional as authentically dramatic, able powerfully to hold the expression of emotion, suffering, conflict.

Marseille Music Hall

'As I was writing *Marius*, I was hearing the voices of the Marseillais actors at the Alcazar', Pagnol recalled. Indeed he was thinking to write 'in the Marseillais genre' and the trilogy emerges from a flourishing local tradition of music-hall and variety theatre. The Alcazar to which he refers was one of the two great Marseille café-concert establishments (the

other was the Palais de Cristal). Both were opened in the latter half of the nineteenth century and both drew large audiences (the Alcazar's was reputed to be decent working-class and petit-bourgeois, somewhat more 'respectable' than that of the Palais). The Alcazar's speciality was revues – *revues Marseillaises*: assemblages of songs and sketches mostly set in Marseille and with character types based on the common people of the city; fish-stall women like Honorine for example.

True to this tradition, the trilogy contains a number of scenes that are themselves really just sketches, only moderately relevant, if at all, to the dramatic action. One such scene in *César* is that in which, despite the reproaches of an astonished M. Brun, the other bar regulars place a rock under a hat in the road and speculate on the enjoyment they will derive from watching passersby take a painful kick at it (M. Brun's initial disapproval is explained, of course, by him not being Marseillais; soon he too becomes caught up in the 'game'). Another is that involving the mix-up of hats in the funeral procession, which leaves a little man at the back sunk under César's very large bowler and César with a diminutive one perched on his pate. Hats, indeed, are called on for various comic effects throughout the trilogy and Marseille 'hat humour' was a commonplace of music-hall stage and Vieux-Port streets. Rarely do observers of the time fail to mention 'the old rite of the hat': in the alleyways where the brothels were found, men were likely to have their hats whisked off and thrown around among the women, often never to be seen again (Benjamin, suggesting perhaps that we see the diminution of César's headgear as a momentary cutting down to size of the domineering patriarch, wondered whether anyone had 'ever probed deeply enough into this refuse heap of houses to reach the innermost place in the gynaeceum, the chamber where the captured emblems of manhood – boaters, bowlers, hunting hats, trilbies, jockey caps – hang in rows on consoles or in layers on racks'). Along with such sketches go the individual comic turns, moments in which a character will do a routine of one sort or another – the Chauffeur's 'God-strike-me-down-if-I-lie' scene with Fanny is an obvious example.

Marius was to be local and Pagnol envisaged that the play would be impossible to stage outside of Marseille (certainly no further away than Avignon or Toulon) and anyway he was after success in Paris as a serious writer. So naturally he offered the play to the director of the Alcazar, who, according to Pagnol, refused it on the grounds that it was too good not to go to a major Paris theatre. Its Parisian success then launched a craze for things Marseillais, a craze consolidated by the play *Fanny* and massively inflated by the trilogy films. In the first years of the 1930s, Marseille songs, variety shows, operettas, plays and films became immensely popular: the celebrated Concert Mayol in Paris began to inject 'the Marseille flavour' into its shows; the popular singer Alibert, a Marseillais whose performances had previously been deliberately Parisian in tone, began to use Marseille material and co-authored *La Revue Marseillaise* in which he starred from April 1932 (he was later to play Marius in the first production of the play *César*); recording companies, which prior to the 1930s had no Marseille/Provençal material in their catalogues, began to record songs and sketches (including sketches featuring Raimu as César in new comic situations); a humorous paper called *Marius* set out to introduce the spirit of the *galéjade* to Paris and published a series of trilogy-inspired almanacs (*Almanach de César*, *Almanach d'Escartefigue*, and so on); Alibert, the librettist René Sarvil and the songwriter Vincent Scotto, another

Marseillais and composer of the music for *César*, together launched the vogue for Marseillais operetta with their *Au Pays du soleil* (1933), followed by a host of others with Marseille-proclaiming titles: *Un de la Canebière*, *Les Gangsters du Château d'If* (1939), *Le Roi des galéjeurs* (1939). All of these and more were turned into films and actors from Marseille and the Midi filled the screens, most of them in one way or another associated with Pagnol.

Marseille Modernity

Escartefigue is captain of the ferry-boat – the *fériboîte* in Marseillais – that from 1880 carried people across the Vieux-Port between the Quai du Port and the Quai de Rive Neuve. In the year of the making of *César*, it was equipped with a diesel motor but the trilogy's boat seems not to have left the age of steam and, becalmed in the past, is suffering from competition: 'It's the Pont Transbordeur that's causing me harm. Before they built that heap of old iron, my boat was always full. Now they all use the Transbordeur ... it's more modern than the *fériboîte*, and they don't get seasick' (the idea that people get seasick during the *fériboîte*'s crossing – all of 206 metres! – leaves Marius incredulous, though

The Transbordeur rises behind the fériboîte in *Fanny*

Escartefigue claims to know at least one person who has been sick: himself!). The *fériboîte* still exists, mainly for tourists, the current boat still named rather inappropriately after the never-on-a-boat bar-owner César.

The heap of iron to which Escartefigue refers was indeed 'more modern'. Built in the first years of the twentieth century at the far – sea – end of the Vieux-Port, the Pont Transbordeur came into service in December 1905. The aim was to link the two sides of the port while leaving shipping freedom of passage. To this end, two tall 'towers' were erected, one on each side, with a walkway between them at the top for pedestrians and a platform lower down – a kind of mobile ferry suspended by cables above the water – capable of supporting considerable weight and on which vehicles and pedestrians could be

The Transbordeur frames images for the night of love and marks time passing

transported, the platform being driven across by two electric motors. As the Eiffel Tower became the symbol of Paris, so the Pont Transbordeur became that of Marseille, the emblematic image of the city, appearing as such at points in the trilogy and also used by Pagnol at certain intense moments to suggest an emotionally charged passage of time (Fanny and Marius's first night of love is the notable example). Like the Eiffel Tower (1887–9), also of course in iron, the Transbordeur employed the most modern forms and techniques of construction to achieve a structure that recast perceptions of the urban space. The startlingly new visual perspectives offered from the high walkway and from within the open iron stairways leading up to it on either side transformed the experience of the city.

In his classic 1928 account of an avant-garde modern architecture, *Bauen in Frankreich, Bauen in Eisen, Bauen in Eisenbeton* (*Building in France, Building in Iron, Building in Ferro-concrete*), the architectural critic Sigfried Giedion took the Pont Transbordeur as a pivotal work: 'This structure ... cannot be excluded from the urban image, whose fantastic crowning it denotes. But its interplay with the city is neither "spatial" nor "plastic". It engenders floating relations and interpenetrations. The boundaries of architecture are blurred.' Benjamin was 'electrified' by Giedion's book which he praised for teaching its readers to see 'the fundamental features of architecture today' and for 'taking the grandiose views offered on the city by constructions in iron such as the Pont Transbordeur as model for the philosopher wishing to discover hitherto unknown points of view'. The book's cover was designed by the Hungarian-born Bauhaus artist Moholy-Nagy and used one of Giedion's

News of the birth of Césariot rings out over the Vieux-Port and the ever-present Transbordeur 75

76   Tim Gidal, *Boats in the Vieux-Port*, 1930 (photo taken from the Transbordeur), © Peter Gidal

Social squalor and optical imaging in Moholy-Nagy's *Impressions of the Old Port of Marseille*   77

own photos of the Transbordeur printed negatively. (Moholy-Nagy was responsible for the design of the book overall, a modernist work in its own right.)

Moholy-Nagy was only one of a number of artists – photographers particularly, such as Germaine Krull, Tim Gidal, Man Ray, Florence Henri, Herbert Bayer – for whom in the 1920s and 30s the Transbordeur embodied modernity and provided a visual source for modernist work. Technology and the changing urban and industrial environment were taken as generating new sensory impressions that demanded new artistic forms dedicated to the active transformation of given, passively reproduced ways of seeing. Moholy-Nagy talked of a 'reeducation of the senses' and the Transbordeur was valued as enabling 'the new vision' that he sought to achieve through his photographic practice. Close-ups creating abstract patterns out of its structures and materials together with vertical perspectives looking down from or up inside it were used to abolish static relations to a comfortably envisioned reality in the interests of 'optical images' that would force people 'to see the objective reality, valid from the optical point of view'. The camera could be made to present spatial and temporal relations inaccessible to the human eye and the Transbordeur was a source for – and the material fact of – such visual transformation.

Moholy-Nagy, moreover, is of special interest here for his use of film to attain the new vision. The cinematic expression of the modernist avant-garde's encounter with Marseille, indeed, was his *Impressionen vom alten Marseiller Hafen* (*Impressions of the Old Port of Marseille*) made in 1929. With eight minutes or so of film at his disposal, Moholy-Nagy, like Pagnol, concentrated on the Vieux-Port area of the city, but, unlike Pagnol, concentrated on it as somewhere 'little-known to the public because of its poor social situation, its misery and its dangerous streets' (he reported having himself often felt in danger there). The film eschews narrative – there is no fiction to *familiarise* the city – and works in contrasts; most evidently moving between a realism of social documentation (the poverty of the streets; 'a sketch of the situation', as Moholy-Nagy put it) and the construction of a mode of seeing in line with his modernist purpose; the viewer's stability of position disturbed by extreme high and low angles, shifting perspectives, flattening of image depth into unsettling formal, 'optical' compositions – much as in his photographs, some of which were used in the film.

The Transbordeur as Marseille
background in *Fanny* ...

... and as glimpse of
modernism in the opening
credits for *César*

The document-images and the film-specific 'mobile spatial
projections' (Moholy-Nagy's term for the creative possibility offered by
film as medium) run alongside and against one another in a film practice
of Marseille evidently at odds with the developing conventions of a
commercial mainstream cinema's use of the city. Moholy-Nagy, we
might say, is at one end of a spectrum which has Escartefigue at the other
with, precisely, the Pont Transbordeur between them, the heap of metal
that is a modernity of Marseille from which the trilogy and Pagnol are
largely in retreat.

CONCLUSION

The play *Marius* was envisaged as 'beaucoup trop local', too local for any but an audience of Marseillais. Pagnol was persuaded otherwise and proved wrong, and then proved wrong again by the success of the trilogy films. Renoir, a self-declared 'internationalist', insisted at the same time on the need for a national cinema and saw Pagnol in the 1930s as a – if not *the* – major contributor to its French development: 'One must show what one knows well' – Renoir's principle, Pagnol's practice. Bazin saw him as France's first *regionalist* film-maker, stressing the *localisation* of his films as determining in their success: 'Pagnol owes his international popularity first of all, paradoxically, to the regionalism of his work.'

The important reference for Renoir and Bazin was to the films of the inland villages and hills: *Angèle* or *Regain* or, in Bazin's case, the later *Manon des sources*. The cinematic landscape of those films, shot largely in exteriors, is different, from the trilogy's world of the Vieux-Port, which is more sociable, more comic, fuller with speech – is, in short, that Pagnolesque 'Marseille'. This leaves the trilogy's films involved in a difficult and shifting balance between the local as end and the local as site of human drama that transcends that thickness of locality which is at the same time the very essence of its films. At any given moment, there is the threat of story and characters miring in local colour, turning picturesque, merely *exemplifying*.

Dependent so closely on its language and its actor-performers, the trilogy was not an easy source for adaptations and remakes by other

cinemas. As mentioned earlier, foreign language versions of *Marius* in German and Swedish were shot alongside the French version and versions of *Fanny* were made in Germany and Italy (the German version starring Emil Jannings as César). Two adaptations were also made in

Wallace Beery, César, and Maureen O'Sullivan, Fanny, in *Port of Seven Seas*

Hollywood, without much success. The first, in 1938, was MGM's *Port of Seven Seas*, directed by James Whale from a Preston Sturges script. The trilogy was condensed into a single film, taking *Fanny* as its main focus and leaving out the narrative resolution found in *César*. Whale's film has Marius returning to sea so as to allow Fanny's – and his – child a stable life and closes with her and Panisse happily admiring their baby's first tooth (!). The film's career, however, was not so happy. Whale was ill at ease at MGM and had problems during the shooting with Wallace Beery, his César. Originally to be called *Madelon*, that being the name given to the Fanny character played by Maureen O'Sullivan (the change was to accommodate American susceptibilities regarding the word 'fanny'), the film was announced for release in April 1938 as *Life on the Waterfront* and finally released in July of that year with its definitive *Port of Seven Seas* title.

The second Hollywood version (Mansfield Productions, with Warner Bros. distribution) was made much later by Joshua Logan, the successful director of the 1958 *South Pacific*, and released in 1961 under the title *Fanny* (American susceptibilities apparently no longer such a problem). This approached the trilogy via the 1954 Broadway musical *Fanny* written by Logan and S. N. Behrman with music by Harold Rome; while not itself made as a musical, its background music score nevertheless incorporated songs from the Broadway production. If some of the film was shot on location in the Vieux-Port, the cast was cosmopolitan, though French-born – but not Marseille-born – Hollywood stars took three of the leading roles: Leslie Caron, Fanny; Charles Boyer, César; and Maurice Chevalier, Panisse; Marius was played by a German, Horst Bucholz (which would have had Raimu apoplectic, he who had been initially furious at the idea of the Parisian Fresnay in the role). Like *Port of Seven Seas*,

Logan's film was also a condensation of the trilogy but this time drawing its material largely from *César*. It begins with Fanny, Panisse and the baby and Marius's return to sea, moves forward nine years to Panisse's death, and from there to the union of Fanny and Marius in fulfilment of Panisse's dying wish. The change in the number of years that have passed – making Césariot a young child rather than a young man – means effectively that much of *César* is eliminated and all the final drama is gone since there is no need for tension, no call for difficult explanations between Césariot and Fanny, Marius and César.

The inclusion of *César* in the BFI's list of 'Film Classics' is perhaps not self-evident – what place can it claim as a classic alongside *Citizen Kane* or *La Grande Illusion* or *L'avventura*? Nor is it perhaps self-evident that it should be *César* rather than another Pagnol film: *Angèle* for example (for Godard, 'one of the finest films ever made' and the Italian neo-realists' acknowledged precursor) or *La Femme du boulanger* (so much admired by Welles). The choice of *César*, however, has its force. The film was a great popular success and the success is also that of its cultural significance, its passage into the national popular culture. Along with the other films of the trilogy, it represents too an important moment in the development of the talking picture and it and Pagnol are significant in the debates surrounding that development. The opposition between theatre and cinema, to which those debates can be too readily constrained, is challenged by *César* which manages theatre filmically and cinema dramatically to give a work which stands as a film. That this is done, that *César* is made, within the context of an

Today's feriboîte, the *César*, approaches the Quai de Rive Neuve; on the other side of the port can be seen the façade of the Hôtêl de Ville where Fanny and Panisse were married

achievement of independence by a director who established himself as a man of cinema all along the line of production, is also part of the historical importance. To cultural and historical importance moreover should be added pleasure. The pathos, the melodrama, can still move, breaking through the screens of ideology, and the occasional over-theatricality of dialogue and acting does not take away from the film's achievement as *a film*.

'One doesn't know what to think of him', was the *Cahiers du cinéma* comment on Pagnol in the 1950s. In an interview in 1977, however, *Cahiers* editor, Serge Daney described 'the cinema *Cahiers* likes – has always liked' as 'a cinema HAUNTED BY WRITING ... This is the key to understanding the magazine's successive tastes and choices. It can be explained too by the fact that the best French film-makers have always been – at the same time – writers.' He offered Pagnol as a key example and *César* without doubt is a quintessential achievement of Pagnol the writer–director, as Welles so rightly described him.

CREDITS

· ·

César

César

France
1936

Director
Marcel Pagnol
Producer
Marcel Pagnol
Screenplay
Marcel Pagnol
Director of Photography
Willy [Faktorovitch]
Editor
Suzanne de Troeye
Sound Engineer
G. Gérardot
Art Director
Galibert
Music
Vincent Scotto

Production Company
Les Films Marcel Pagnol
Production Manager
Charles Pons
**Assistant Production
Managers**
Léon Bourelly
Jean Adam
Fernand Bruno
**Second Camera
Operators**
Roger Ledru
Gricha [Charly Grégoire
Faktorovitch]
Assistants
Pierre Méré
Pierre Arnaudy
**Assistant Sound
Engineers**
Julien Coutellier
Bañuls
Grips/Gaffers
Albert Spanna
Antoine Rossi
Assistant Grips/Gaffers
Joseph Latière
Henri Garcia
Michel Scotto
Francillon

Set Designer
Marius Brouquier
Furniture
Maison David Frères
Make-up
Constanzo Albino
Orchestra Conductor
Georges Sellers
Laboratory Supervisor
Albert Assouad
Laboratory Assistants
Clément Maure
Le Van Kim
André Robert
Developing and Printing
Laboratoires des Films
Marcel Pagnol, Marseille
Sound Recording
Voisin et Cie
Sound Process
G. I. Kraemer

Cast
[Jules] Raimu
César [Ollivier]
Pierre Fresnay
Marius [Ollivier]
[Fernand] Charpin
Maître Honoré Panisse
Orane Demazis
Fanny [Cabanis]
André Fouché
Césariot Panisse
Alida Rouffe
Honorine [Cabanis]
Milly Mathis
Tante Claudine [Foulon]
Robert Vattier
Monsieur [Aldebert] Brun
Paul Dullac
[Félix] Escartefigue
[Marcel] Maupi
'Le Chauffeur'
[Innocent Mangiapan]
Édouard Delmont
Doctor Félicien Venelle
[Louis Alfred] Doumel
Fernand
Thommeray
Elzéar, the priest of St Victor
Jean Castan
L'Enfant de chœur

[Robert] Bassac
Pierre Dromart [Dromard in
some text editions of *César*]
Rellys
Panisse's employee
Charblay
Henri, owner of the bar in
Toulon
Odette Roger
Hotel chambermaid
Albert Spanna
Postman

Black and White
10,500 feet
117 minutes
[see discussion in text pp. 26–7]

The three trilogy films are
issued on VHS cassette and
DVD by the Compagnie
Méditerranéenne de Films.

Credits checked by
Markku Salmi

BIBLIOGRAPHICAL NOTE

· ·

Pagnol's works are collected in three volumes: *Oeuvres complètes*, Paris: Editions de Fallois 1995; volume I contains his plays (including *Marius* and *Fanny* and the prefaces to them); volume II his cinema (including *César* in the 'film de 1936' version, together with a preface; as also a version of the 'Cinématurgie de Paris' articles); volume III his memoirs and novels. The texts of the plays *Marius* and *Fanny* and of the film *César* (the same 'film de 1936' version) are available singly in paperback in the Editions de Fallois 'Collection Fortunio', Paris, 1988. The earlier text version of the film was published by Fasquelle, Paris, 1937, and the play *César* was published in *Réalités*, Série littéraire et théâtrale no. 1, Paris 1947. Quotations from Pagnol are taken largely from the original *Cahiers du film* 'Cinématurgie de Paris' articles, from the prefaces mentioned above, and from interviews with him conducted by Pierre Tchernia in six television programmes broadcast in 1973 under the title *Morceaux choisis* and available through the Institut National de l'Audiovisuel. Roger Richebé's *Au-delà de l'écran*, Monte Carlo, Pastorelly, 1977, fascinating in its own right, contains the Aunt Zoë scene omitted from *Fanny*.

Jean Renoir is quoted from the collection of his writings published as *Écrits 1926–1971*, Paris, Pierre Belfon, 1974; René Clair's account of his arguments with Pagnol can be found in *Cinéma d'hier, cinéma d'aujourd'hui*, 'Collection Idées', Paris: Gallimard, 1970; Orson Welles's comment on Pagnol as writer–director is from Mark W. Estrin (ed.), *Orson Welles: Interviews*, Jackson: University Press of Mississippi, 2002; and Godard's regarding Pagnol's troupe from Alain Bergala (ed.), *Jean-Luc Godard par Jean-Luc Godard*, vol. 1, Paris: Cahiers du cinéma, 1998. André Bazin's 'Le Cas Pagnol' can now most easily be found in the 'definitive edition' of *Qu'est-ce que le cinéma?*, Paris: Éditions du Cerf, 2002. Walter Benjamin's two pieces on Marseille, 'Marseille' (1929) and 'Haschisch in Marseille' (1932), are in his *Gesammelte Schriften* vol. IV.1, Frankfurt am Main, Suhrkamp, 1972, in translation in Michael W. Jennings, Howard Eiland and Gary Smith (eds), *Selected Writings* vol. 2, Cambridge, MA, Belknap Press, 1999. Siegfried Kracauer's piece, 'Zwei Flächen' ('Two Surfaces') (1926) is in his *Aufsätze 1915–1926, Schriften*, vol. 5.1, Frankfurt am Main, Suhrkamp, 1990. Giedion is quoted from Sigfried Giedion, *Bauen in Frankreich, Bauen in Eisen, Bauen in Eisenbeton*, Leipzig, 1928; translated as *Building in France, Building in*

Iron, Building in Ferro-concrete, Santa Monica: Getty Center for the History of Art and the Humanities, 1995. Contemporary accounts of Marseille cited are: Albert Londres, *Marseille: Porte du Sud*, Paris: Éditions de France, 1926, and Alfred Suarès, *Marsiho*, Paris: M. P. Trémois, 1931. The *Cahiers du cinéma* survey referred to in the Introduction is 'Soixante metteurs en scène français', May 1957, and Serge Daney's comment quoted in the Conclusion is from his *La Maison cinéma et le monde*, vol. 1, Paris, P.O.L., 2001. Raymond Chirat and Olivier Barrot are quoted from their *Les Excentriques du cinéma français (1929–1958)*, Paris: Henri Veynier, 1985. The biography of Pagnol by Raymond Castans has been of much assistance: *Marcel Pagnol*, Paris: Jean-Claude Lattès, 1987.

Material concerning Marseille at the time of the trilogy is mostly derived from work on a different but related project in the Archives Départementales des Bouches-du-Rhône and I should like to acknowledge the friendly and efficient help given by the staff there.

PICTURE CREDITS

Marius (Films Marcel Pagnol, 1931); *Fanny* (Films Marcel Pagnol, 1932); *Angèle* (Société des Films Marcel Pagnol, 1934); *La Fille du puisatier* (Société des Films Marcel Pagnol, 1940); *Topaze* (Société des Films Marcel Pagnol, 1950); *Fièvre* (Alhambra Films, 1921); *Cœur fidèle* (Pathé-Consortium-Cinema, 1923); *Impressionen vom alten Marseiller Hafen* (1929; Munich Film Museum); *Justin de Marseille* (Pathé-Natan, 1934); *Le Club des fadas* (1938); *Port of Seven Seas* (Loew's Incorporated, 1938); *Le Garçon sauvage* (Films Gibé,1951); [Joshua Logan's] *Fanny* (Mansfield Productions, 1961); *Cap Canaille* (Babylone Films, 1983); *À Bout de souffle* (Société Nouvelle de Cinématographie, 1959).

ALSO PUBLISHED

If you would like further information about future BFI Film Classics or about other books on film, media and popular culture from BFI Publishing, please write to:
BFI Film Classics
BFI Publishing
21 Stephen Street
London W1T 1LN

05190747